VILLAS AND GARDENS
OF TUSCANY

Text by Sophie Bajard
Photographs by Raffaello Bencini

TERRAIL

CONTENTS

The fishpond with the mask
Villa Pratolino

Front cover:
Villa Centinale

Back cover:
The gardens of Villa Garzoni

Editors: Jean-Claude Dubost and Jean-François Gonthier
Art director: Bernard Girodroux
English adaptation: Frances Wister Faure
with Eugène Clarence Braun-Munk
Composition & filmsetting: Compo Rive Gauche

© FINEST S.A./ÉDITIONS PIERRE TERRAIL, PARIS 1993
ISBN: 2-87939-059-1
Printed in Italy

FOREWORD

Who is not reminded of Tuscany while looking at the landscapes in the background of paintings by Perugino, Raphael or Leonardo da Vinci? Who is not suddenly transported to the Tuscan countryside with its rolling hills shimmering in the blue light of dawn, crossed by delicate streams and paths bordered by tall silhouettes of cypress trees? Who has not felt a sudden longing to reside there in some quiet retreat and lead a peaceful and contemplative life?

Few are fortunate enough to experience this happiness; we had the pleasure of meeting some of them during our peregrinations. Choosing from among the scores of villas has been a difficult task. Already in the 16th century the great Florentine historian, Benedetto Varchi expressed his amazement over the large number of villas scattered about the Tuscan hills. Today, they literally cover the slopes. The selection presented here is therefore a mere sample of the treasures that embellish the Florentine countryside. We have made an effort to convey the geographical, sociological, cultural, political and economic diversity of these villas, and to bring out the artistic significance of this region, with its three noteworthy centers: Florence, Lucca and Siena. We made our choice simply from the fondness we felt for the site, from what we had enthusiastically read on the subject and from the advice of friends. Often, it was simply thanks to our haphazard wanderings. Raffaello Bencini and I followed our instincts and our fancies. This book owes much to our association and to our common interests. I remain very much indebted to him for his good will and constant concern.

Fortunately, Tuscany has kept its age-old tradition of hospitality, offering us unending warmth and welcome. Even the owners of private villas accept to serve as guides to amateur art-lovers when they show a sincere interest. Whether members of the old Tuscan aristocracy, newer middle-class families, or well-to-do foreigners, the owners have all—for reasons of comfort and expediency—altered the villas to some extent, but have always succeeded in preserving the charm of former times. I now know for sure that a Tuscan villa has never been acquired by accident. Having explored this glorious region and entered so many superb estates not open to the usual tourist circuits, I had the opportunity of meeting people of profound culture, true enthusiasts who are passionately expansive about their houses and gardens, and about Tuscany as a whole. I would like to dedicate to them the remark made by the late owner of Villa I Tatti's, Bernard Berenson, who said: "I wonder whether art has a higher function than to make us feel, appreciate and enjoy natural objects for their art value?"

Olive groves
and the Chianti hills
surrounding Villa Cetinale.

HISTORICAL OUTLINE

SOCIAL FUNCTIONS OF THE TUSCAN VILLA

The phenomenal proliferation of villas across Italy since the early Renaissance can only be understood when placed in the proper social, economical and political context. In the 12th century, Florence began to extend its domination to other Tuscan towns such as Arezzo, Fiesole, Pistoia, Pisa and Prato. The rise of the wool and silk industries brought significant development to the region. The textile industry scattered its production throughout rural areas, generating new residential hubs all around the countryside. In order to feed the growing population, the Florentine oligarchy began to exploit the resources of the land and created a more balanced urban-rural relationship in the process. The rising *bourgeoisie* established smaller properties among the fragmented feudal estates of the aristocracy. These *case da signore* (manor houses), accompanied by their indispensable *case da lavatore* (share-cropper dwellings) and *case coloniche* (farm houses), shared the land with the age-old fortified castles.

During the 13th and 14th centuries, Tuscany experienced a period of intensive commercial activity well managed by a hardy group of entrepreneurs. Whether from the old nobility or *nouveau riche*, these new patricians developed the same business practices and had the same sort of lifestyle. The aggressive merchant families of Florence were the most adept bankers in Europe thanks to their hard currency, the florin. They bought and sold commodities, exchanged coins, invested in businesses, granted loans, etc. They also manufactured, bought and sold textiles (woolen, cotton and linen fabrics, silks and brocades…), engaged in agriculture (citrus fruits, vegetables, oils, spices…) and produced, luxury items (furs, jewelry, silverware, tapestries, paintings) and raw material (lead, iron). In those days, most Tuscan entrepreneurs also invested in real estate, buying or building houses in the city and in the neighboring countryside. On occasion they foreclosed their clients' mortgaged properties when the latter could not pay off their loans. It would, however, be erroneous to attribute this accumulation of wealth simply to ostentation; these were in fact safe, long-term investments. Behind the shadow of each Tuscan patrician lurked a clever businessman.

What better example than the Medici family. Their enterprise, a mercantile operation, was created in 1397 by Giovanni di Bicci and then run by his son Cosimo the Elder, until the latter's death in 1464. Today we would call it a conglomerate. In addition to banking facilities, it included one silk and two wool concerns in Florence. Cosimo the elder covered Latin Christendom with a network of subsidiary branches: Pisa, Rome, Venice, Milan, Avignon, Bruges, London and Geneva. He took over papal banking and became the official tax collector for the Holy See. His firm traded with the Ottoman Empire and the Levant while it did business with European kings and princes, lending them large sums of money.

The Tuscan villa, situated at the center of a vast estate, remained bound to its agricultural vocation. After the abolition of serfdom in the 13th century, a system of sharecropping developed throughout Italy. In this period, however, few peasants succeeded in becoming or remaining property owners. It was these sharecroppers who cultivated the land, produced the basic foods, tended the herds and the fishponds, kept up the orchards, planted the vegetable gardens and harvested the olive groves and vineyards for the benefit of the owners of the villas. The produce was most often exported throughout Italy, if not, all over Europe. The villa was expected to provide sufficient income to sustain the landlord's family living in the city as well as all the peasants toiling the soil. The overseer and the sharecroppers lived on the property in poor hovels which they often shared with their domestic animals. The owner entrusted the management of the estate to the overseer,

View of Florence and the olive
groves on the Settignano hillsides
from Villa Gamberaia.

Above:
View from the terrace
of Villa Gamberaia

seldom being present himself, except on brief visits to verify the accounts and inspect the produce. It was only during the summer season that the villa became an appealing place for recreation and leisure.

At the end of the 14th century, Tuscany entered into a period of even more intense capitalistic activity. The entrepreneurs diversified their interests and engaged in a wide variety of ventures, assuming the roles of merchant, transporter, banker, moneychanger, insurance broker and manufacturer. Because of the increasing size of their business network, they had to delegate even more responsibility to their agents; they began to handle business from company headquarters and gradually gave up traveling to distant trading posts.

As the merchants and bankers became more and more sedentary, their frame of mind changed. Encouraged by their new social status, they indulged in philanthropy and turned to the Arts to display their wealth and power. With fortunes gained by their business skills, they began to commission the great architects of the day—Michelozzo Michelozzi, Leon Battista Alberti, Giuliano da Sangallo—to build or refurbish their town and country houses. Their patronage brought fame and glory, while securing the means to express the ideas and values of this new class, called the "learned merchants." Their Villas soon began to sprout on hills of Tuscany. In 1472, they already numbered 3,600, with a total value of 14 million ducats. The aim of these men, who promoted the emergence of the Humanistic Movement in Italy, was to recapture the ideals and beauty of Antiquity, and to go deeper into their knowledge of Man. Aspiring to individual perfection, they devoted their time to more spiritual pursuits and showed a marked preference for the life of a country gentleman. They felt the need for a bucolic and serene place of rest—the country villa. There, cloistered in small, hidden secret gardens, far from the tumult of the city, they rediscovered the teachings of the ancient Roman authors, Pliny, Seneca, Columella and of course Virgil who idealized a rural type of life in his *Georgics*, close to nature and conducive to contemplation. The villa became the image of a worldly "Lost Paradise," the promise of a wholesome life devoted to agriculture. Lorenzo the Magnificent, in such inspired poems as *Nencia de Barbero*, sung praises of the peasant's happy life. He adopted a pastoral-style architecture for Careggi, the villa that was to become the home of the Neo-Platonic Academy under the auspices of his friend, the philosopher Marsilio Ficino. There, Ficino and other great Humanists such as Pico della Mirandola and Politian, rediscovered and translated works by Plato and his disciples. Many treatises describing the characteristics of the villa and explaining its function were written at the time by the likes of Leon Battista Alberti, Anton Francesco Doni, G. Falcone, A. Gallo and Petrarch.

The early 16th century brought changes to the entrepreneur's situation. For one thing, the wars tearing Italy apart caused an economic disaster that did not spare the region; then, merchants of Tuscany were forced to keep up with tough competition from Spain and Portugal (especially on the American continent) and from the new textile industries in Venice, Milan and France and England. In 1512, after the death of Pandolfo Petrucci, who had been in power since 1487, a period of political ferment ensued. The crisis in the Sienese government, the exile of the Medici from Florence in 1494, the republican interlude and the short reign of Alexander de' Medici all contributed to the unrest.

Peace and order were restored by Cosimo I after his election to the head of the Florentine government in 1537, and the Grand-Duchy of Tuscany, which encompassed the Republic of Siena (1557), was created. Cosimo I enforced new measures to protect the poorer classes from the famines that frequently prevailed in the region: he forbade the export of agricultural produce from the Grand Duchy, regulated the circulation of goods within the territory, set prices and built public storage to house supplies, modified the administrative and judiciary systems, and created a new influential class of civil servants chosen among the petty bourgeois and the old noble families. These privileged few began to invest their money in land, a more secure way to safeguard their accumulated profits than speculations in commercial ventures. All these measures, however, had the long-term effect of bringing agricultural growth to a standstill. For example, identical policies prohibiting the export of raw materials and the import of manufactured articles were applied to the wool and silk industries. This more or less disastrous decision generated serious economic and financial difficulties for the merchant oligarchy who, in turn, invested in real estate.

Cosimo I also encouraged a general exodus to the country, thinking that this might contain the increasing political power of the business class. In 1562, he founded a military order, the Knights of St. Stephen, ostensibly to protect Tuscan transports and caravans from being attacked by Turkish pirates, but in fact, designed to keep the merchants away from their businesses. As compensation, Cosimo awarded them with titles and land. This re-feudalization trend led to a blossoming of new country villas which would be used for residence at least part of the year, during the summer and fall seasons. In less than fifty years, the number of villas increased tenfold; in 1520, there were thirty-two thousand in the vicinity of Florence alone. Many artists and artisans were called on to restore and embellish old edifices that seemed too austere for their new owners. The main function of this new type of villa, both luxurious and spacious, was no longer to be farming; the pleasantness of rural life was a thing of the past and seclusion no longer sought. The villa had become a place for gracious living and entertainment—a symbol of social status.

This lifestyle continued throughout the 16th and 17th centuries. Ferdinand I, carrying on the economic policies of his predecessor with a true mercantile appetite, granted the Medici family the monopoly on the trade of grains cultivated on such different Medicean properties as Careggi and Poggio a Caiano. The newly ennobled businessmen set up limited partnerships in foreign countries and invested their money in Tuscan real estate. With the ownership of feudal properties came many privileges in both the civil and judicial spheres: hunting and fishing rights, the right to levy taxes… Members of this wealthy elite led the high social life of courtiers and accumulated property for several generations until they possessed most of the land. The villa season lasted all year round with the exception of the mid-winter months. The country houses were enlivened by the same kinds of entertainment, costly banquets, and flamboyant receptions, as the *palazzi*.

In 1815, after the Napoleonic period, the House of Lorraine regained the throne of the Grand Duchy of Tuscany they had once occupied. The European intellectual world was then dominated by the Romantic Movement with its emphasis on feeling, originality and empathy with nature. A renewed vogue for antiquity and ruins inspired travelers—writers and artists—mostly English, Dutch and German—to wander around Italy, savoring the perfume of the mythical cradle of Western civilization. Falling in love with Tuscany, they finally settled there and bought many of the villas, preserving their Renaissance character, while enriching them with collections of paintings, sculpture and art objects of all kinds worthy of a museum. The villa became their principal place of residence and once again, the Italians worn out by a hectic city life, followed suit.

Today, the people who choose to live in Tuscan villas come from many different backgrounds, and they have made this choice for specific reasons. All, whether natives or newcomers, are attracted by the ethereal light and the natural beauty of the land so skillfully transformed by man's ingenuity. Although the social function of the Tuscan villa has changed considerably over the centuries, the environment and a certain life-style were created six hundred years ago.

SETTING FOR THE TUSCAN VILLA

Since Antiquity, the choice of site for a villa has been a matter of great importance, not only for aesthetic considerations like the view, but also for practical reasons like health and comfort. In the 14th century, a special theory on the ideal placement for a villa was set forth with regard to layout, architecture and landscaping. This concept, influenced by Humanism and Pastoralism, was based for the most part on Pliny the Younger's estate in Tusculum, *Il Laurentino*. Pliny expressed his views on the subject in a letter to his friend, Domitius Apollinarius. He did not describe the architecture of the ideal house in detail, but commented on the loving care which should be taken while planning each room in relation to the garden and landscape, on the use of space during every season of the year and on the

The park at Villa Cafaggiolo.

Above:
View from the tower of Il Trebbio
over the terrace bordered with
cypress trees and, in the distance,
the Mugello valley.

general atmosphere of the house. In 1485, Leon Battista Alberti, the great Florentine Humanist and architect, expounded in great detail in the fifth book of his *De Re Aedificatoria* (dedicated to Lorenzo the Magnificent) on the best ways to choose a site for a villa. Clearly, a hilly site best suited his interpretation of classical antiquity. His recommendations conveniently coincided with the fact that the castles in Tuscany had been built on hilltops, and so could be used as the foundation on which to rebuild a villa designed according to the latest Renaissance fashion. The most important condition for Alberti was that the site be in harmony with nature. It should be part of an agricultural estate, situated on fertile soil and, if possible, near thick woods, and chosen for the pleasantness of the country air and general climate, the sweetness of the fields and the safety of the neighborhood. The master's house should be built facing the rising sun at the equinox, in an open spot with pleasant vistas, but sheltered by surrounding hills. The house should look out over the farm yards, the outbuildings and the cultivated fields in order to have everything in sight. The villa must have an adequate water supply and be able to feed all of its occupants. It should include housing for the peasants, a barn for the oxen, stables, a sheepfold, presses for olives and wine, a cellar, a winter garden, a mill, a loft and storage space. It should be close enough to a city so that its produce can be easily transported to market. The owner should take advantage of the forests and streams for hunting and fishing, not only for the exercise, but to provide sustenance for his family.

An elevated site reaped many advantages; besides giving a beautiful panorama, it represented a symbolic domination over the ordinary mortals living and working below. In Alberti's words: "I do not think it necessary for the Gentlemen's House to stand in the most fruitful Part of his whole Estate but rather in the most Honorable where he can, uncontrolled, enjoy all the Pleasures and Conveniences of Air, Sun, and fine Prospects..."

In order to comply with these recommendations, large tracts of land were needed to accommodate a villa; Il Trebbio, Cafaggiolo and Careggi all spread over more than 25 acres. A basic axial plan emphasized the prospect from the entrance gate to the villa, and from there to the gardens. All the necessary elements that compose a villa were organized hierarchically around the master's house: chapel, terraces, parterres, fountains, pergolas, vegetable beds, orchards, outbuildings, farmhouses, cottages, yards, woods and arable land beyond.

ARCHITECTURE AND DECORATION

Originally, the country villa hardly differed from the farms that still dot the Tuscan countryside. The master's house, the overseer's and the peasants dwellings, and the dependencies were closely grouped into a compact block around a courtyard. This disposition allowed the 12th-century landowner to keep close watch over his possessions and provided a stronghold in case of trouble. Ramparts encircled some of these country places. Watch towers surmounted others, and battlements here and there were not uncommon reminders of the fortified castles of feudal times.

The master's residence was laid out along the same plan as the old Roman villa with not more than four or five different rooms surrounding an interior courtyard (atrium), adorned with a portico (peristyle) on the ground-floor level. Narrow winding stairs led up to a loggia overlooking a small sheltered garden. Most walls were white washed, the floors laid with bricks and beamed ceilings simply decorated with ornamental motifs... The focus was on family life and there was no attempt to impress the occasional visitor.

During the 14th and 15th centuries, although the Tuscan villa was enlarged and improved aesthetically, it retained its austere, somewhat grim appearance, thanks to the influence of Michelozzo Michelozzi in particular. The famous architect of the Medici palazzo in Florence was summoned by Cosimo the Elder to transform the medieval castles of Il Trebbio, Cafaggiolo, Careggi and Fiesole into livable residences more in keeping with the new spirit of the times. Michelozzo used the same model for each with few variations, and did little to change the overall structure of the massive central blocks with their battlements, but added lightness and grace by cutting a small number of openings. The

Giuliano da Sangallo's portico projecting from the façade of Villa Poggio a Caiano.

Above:
Villa Il Trebbio surrounded by wooded hills, the former hunting grounds of the Medici family.

standard plan consisted of a compact edifice surmounted by towers, with a U-shaped façade, preceded by a portico enclosing a central courtyard surrounded by a double loggia. By conserving the fortifications and other medieval protective features, the architect met the Medici's needs for security and allowed them to show off their strength, thus reinforcing their shaky hold over Florence. These refurbished, semi-fortified dwellings were less than aesthetic architectural achievements, but they did answer practical needs.

It was at this time that Leon Battista Alberti outlined, in his *De Re Aedificatoria,* the essential rules of proportion and balance according to the theories of ancient Roman authors like Vitruvius. In Alberti's words, with the disposition of the house "exactly answering the middle of your courtyard, place your entrance with a handsome vestibule, neither narrow, difficult nor obscure. Let the first room that offers itself be a chapel dedicated to God with its Altar. ...from the courtyard we proceed to the parlors which must be contrived for different seasons, some to be used in summer others in winter. Vitruvius says that in winter parlors it is ridiculous to adorn the ceiling with a handsome painting because it will be presently spoilt by the constant smoke of the chimneys. Then come bedchambers and lastly the private rooms for the particular uses of each person in the family. ...the kitchen ought to be neither just under the noses of the guests nor at too great a distance... I think that the apartments of the ladies ought to be sacred like places dedicated to religion and charity." He then went on to recommend flattening the ground around the central block.

Lorenzo's favorite architect, Giuliano da Sangallo, faithfully applied Alberti's principles to Poggio a Caiano, and the villa is a perfect example of the architectural ideals of a 15th-century Humanist. Sangallo successfully operated the progressive transition between the house and the garden by setting the edifice on an arcaded terrace. He was the first to forego the traditional interior courtyard by transforming it into a vaulted hall, thus creating a new area for family gatherings and receptions. To harmonize the overall appearance of the façade, he designed a portico screened by graceful Ionic columns, rather than the former heavy octagonal pillars topped by leafy capitals. He symmetrically distributed all the moldings, doors and window frames and marked them with *pietra serena*, the gray stone of Florence.

The Tuscan villa continued to evolve architecturally; the various stories were clearly separated by cornices, and the central entrance-way framed by rustication; the interior staircase was larger and easier to mount thanks to its stone banister; the rooms were decorated from floor to ceiling with mythological, historical or bucolic scenes, painted by the great artists of the period (Pontormo, Bronzino, Andrea del Sarto, Alessandro Allori); the furnishings, graced by oriental rugs, were grander and became an important feature; the floors were covered with majolica tiles or varnished red bricks from Impruneta.

This type of architecture was reproduced and developed throughout the 16th century by Bernardo Buontalenti, the architect and military engineer of the Medici rulers, Francesco I and Ferdinand I. Buontalenti was the astute inventor of theater decor, hydraulic systems and automatons, in addition to being the architect of the Villa Medici and the Boboli Gardens in Florence. He designed the villas of La Magia, Pratolino, La Petraia, Artimino, Ambrogiana and Leppeggi for the same patrons. Pratolino was copied directly from Poggio a Caiano. Under the impetus of the new ruling class, the villa having now adopted a rational and public-oriented architecture, was filled with guests on holidays and receptions. The architects laid out several different types of plans (with a U-, L-, H- or T-shape), joining several wings that opened out onto the garden. The first story had an open loggia from which the garden could be admired. The double staircase outside, with its banisters, was designed to impress visitors. Buontalenti reconstructed many of the original fortifications, but the old ramparts became terraces for strolling, and the watch towers, belvederes. The owner spent more of his time in his newly refurbished comfort, often accompanied by friends, and it became normal for him to flaunt his wealth. The house took on a more refined Mannerist style and was adorned with many motifs in *pietra serena*, scattered along the façades (consoles, statuary, architraves, pediments, cornices). The outbuildings were set further away from the master's house.

The typically Baroque ceiling decorated with stucco and frescos at Villa Rospigliosi.

Villa Celle's romantic woods,
enhanced by
contemporary sculpture.

These tendencies increased in the 17th century, which saw the rise of a ruling dynasty and its court. Life in the villa was now ordered around the duties of public office and a need was felt for more reception rooms. Ballrooms and banquet halls were added, the inner courtyard was covered with a skylight roof to create an pleasant sun-filled drawing room. Staircases became monumental, grand enough to impress even the most venerable visitor. Guest rooms and dressing rooms were installed for the same reason, obliging owners to add extra floors to the building; these different rooms were oriented according to their exposure to the sun. Thus the bedrooms and libraries were turned towards the East to have the morning light, and the dining room towards the West so that it would remain cool during the day and enjoy the last rays of the sun in the evening. The other rooms were arranged according to the seasons. The summer rooms faced North and the winter rooms, South. It was now in good taste to display one's wealth openly. A veritable plethora of luxury invaded the houses in the form of statues, draperies, objets d'art and ornamentation of all kinds. Trompe-l'œil frescos, columns and cornices generated an architectonic decor with illusionist perspectives and theatrical effects. This was at the height of the Baroque. On the outside, pediments, pilasters, niches, banisters, balconies, and coats of arms were added to the façades. A play of colors came into fashion; the ocher rendering of the walls and the gray highlights of the *pietra serena* harmonized with the tones of stone and marble statuary that graced the garden.

GARDENS AND WOODS

The main concern of a medieval garden was to meet the needs of the household and produce vegetables and fruits such as cherries, peaches, apricots, plums, pears, medlars, pomegranates, figs, almonds, oranges, lemons and so on. Nevertheless, by the middle of the 13th century, the master of a *casa da signore* arranged to have a small enclosed garden adjacent to his country house in order to find rest after a long day. The garden, while keeping its utilitarian character, began to be appreciated for its beauty. With the advent of Humanism, writers and poets rediscovered the symbolism of the Garden of Eden as the paradisiac birthplace of life. In 1350, Boccaccio, the author of the celebrated *Decameron,* praised the marvels of the *giardino segreto* or secret garden, inspired by ancient Roman models that were based essentially on an geometric layout. The Tuscan garden of the early Renaissance, however, remained simple. Besides orchards, beds of vegetables and flower-starred lawns that survived from the medieval period, the garden consisted of a plot of ground divided by several unpaved walks among ornamental parterres bordered by orange and lemon trees in large terra cotta pots. It could be enhanced by a small stone or marble fountain surmounted by a statuette, a fishpond, a vine- or rose-covered pergola, benches and bowers. In some instances, a patch was planted with fragrant herbs and medicinal plants such as juniper, rosemary, bay, myrtle, etc. The garden progressively became a place for enjoyment and contemplation.

In the 15th century, gardeners rediscovered the art of pruning boxwood, yews, cypress and ilex trees into geometrical shapes to form walls of greenery around the parterres and trained especially-planted trees to make foliage roofs over walks with interlacing branches. The Dominican monk, Franceso Colonna, inspired by the Pliny's description of his garden in Tusculum, wrote a mysterious and esoteric book called *Hypnerotomachia Poliphili (Strife of Love in a Dreame),* in which story takes place on the Utopian island of Cytherea where Poliphilus and the lady-of-his-dreams meet Venus. Colonna not only described an ideal garden in his imaginary and fantastic narrative, he also illustrated it with precise drawings engraved in wood, which were widely circulated and profoundly influenced gardening in the 16th century.

It was during this period that the art of topiary invaded the Tuscan garden. Nature was tamed and bridled. Greenery was trimmed into the shape of battlements or animals to provide theatrical backdrops of foliage or to form intricate mazes and imaginatively patterned parterres. Walks bordered with geometrically-clipped box bushes created unforgettable artificial vistas. Stone elements began to appear among the greenery: grottos made of pumice or tufa laden with seashells, mossy imitation rocks, fountains, cascades and ornate ponds with sprays, pavements of pebble mosaics, mythological statues, busts, colonnades and belvederes further embellished the gardens. An "artificial Nature" held sway. The garden, as well as the house, was designed along strict geometrical principles using simple forms such as squares, rectangles, circles and semi-circles. The grounds were divided into different sections, arranged independently and distributed symmetrically along a central axis. A network of rectilinear paths crisscrossed the garden, recalling the *pietra serena* patterns on the façade. Sloping sites were used advantageously by leveling off the terrain into successive terraces enclosed by high retaining walls. Each level permitted the creation of monumental staircases, especially those with a double-flight of steps, as in the Luccan villas of Torrigiani and Garzoni. This type of garden, called *pensile* (hanging garden) faced the surrounding landscape. From the loggia situated higher than the enclosing wall, a view not only of the garden but also of the thickly-wooded hills, could be enjoyed. "Sacred woods" inhabited by nymphs and satyrs have symbolized the home of the gods since Antiquity. Cedars of Lebanon, umbrella pines, fir, elm, ilex and plane trees could be found in these woods and the unruly undergrowth was tamed only by paths.

The double stairs with symmetrical flights at Villa Torrigiani.

This great garden art of the Renaissance attained a kind of perfection and was followed by a period of great popularity. It inspired many imitations during the 17th and 18th centuries but the so-called Italian formal garden lacked originality. It began to borrow some of the characteristics of the classical French garden, with parterres no longer shaped in geometrical patterns, but adopting curvilinear lines, or "embroidery" parterres. In many cases, fantasy was overstated and complexity exaggerated. The species of plants became increasingly varied through the use of cuttings imported from abroad. The size of the gardens increased, some at the expense of their symmetry.

In the 19th century, owners of Tuscan villas began to convert their gardens to adapt to the new fashions imported from England and France. The scores of English who began to colonize the hillsides around Florence hastened the destruction of the old gardens. These recent amateurs of the Italian countryside, untouched by the Humanistic ideals of the Renaissance, heedlessly created gardens according to their own taste. Curiously enough, the Italians themselves were influenced by this trend towards the English style and sacrificed their own gardens without a second thought. A new school of gardeners tore out the parterres, seeded vast lawns, mapped out winding paths in no particular pattern and planted scattered groves that formed elements entirely foreign to the Tuscan climate and soil. The English also introduced flowering plants such as the camellia, the azalea, the rhododendron, the wisteria and the Banks rose (these last two species were used as creepers for pergolas). Not surprisingly, few unaltered Renaissance or Baroque gardens are to be found near Florence today. Villa Celle, for example, acquired a toy lake with miniature rocky and wooded islands, neoclassic urns and columns, bridges over streams and a Gothic Revival chapel—all designed without regard for symmetry. Romantic inventions such as these contrasted with the principles of the formal Italian garden.

At the beginning of this century, however, it was the English who became concerned with the return to the original formal layouts. The landscape gardeners Cecil Pinsent and Geoffrey Scott in Villa I Tatti, and owners like Arthur Acton at La Pietra, reintroduced the formal Italian garden to Tuscany. Soon, Italian landscape architects such as Martino and Pietro Porcinai followed suit and redesigned the Gamberaia, Il Roseto and L'Apparita gardens.

Unlike its Venetian and Roman counterparts, the Tuscan garden's size remained modest and followed the general topography of the land. The artful use of prospects often gave the illusion of distance. The Tuscan garden was characterized by a preponderance of greenery and water over stone and marble. There was a balance between the "artificial Nature" of the man-made garden and the "natural Nature" of untouched woods. Even the large gardens at Pratolino inspired a feeling of intimacy.

Today, the Tuscan villa remains faithful to its 14th-century image as a place of rest, tranquillity and privacy. Hidden in the hills behind high walls or a thick curtain of trees to protect it from intruders, it is often hard to reach and for this reason is veiled in an aura of mystery that incites curiosity and wonder. It reveals its treasures at the price of overcoming many obstacles. Only if you have an adventurous spirit will you be able to discover its jealously-guarded secrets.

DISCOVERING THE VILLAS

NEAR FLORENCE

MEDICI VILLAS

The selection in this book represents only a portion of the villas built by different architects for different members of the Medici family between 1451 and 1591. The first Medicean villas, Il Trebbio and Cafaggiolo, were the centers of vast agricultural domains in the Mugello region, where the origins of the Medici family can be traced back to the 12th century. Cosimo the Elder had been ruling Florence since 1429 when he moved outside the city to Villa Careggi for reasons of safety. At the end of the 15th century, more confident of their supremacy, the Medici acquired properties somewhat more distant from Florence, at Poggio a Caiano and Castello. Chased from their land by the armies of the French king, Charles VIII, the Florentine family only returned to power in 1530 thanks to the help of their Imperial and Pontifical allies. Cosimo I founded the Grand Duchy of Tuscany and continued to expand the family holdings by annexing La Petraia and Poggio Imperiale. At the height of the family's glory, Francesco I de' Medici carried on his father's work and had Villa Pratolino constructed. In the 16th century, the Medici were able to transfer their entire court from one estate to another, according to the weather, the hunting season or other leisurely pursuits.

In 1598, Ferdinand I de' Medici commissioned the Flemish artist Giusto Utens, working in Carrara at the time, to paint a series of lunettes representing all of the Medici villas. These were hung in the grand salon of the Villa Artimino. Recently, in 1969, they were sold at the same time

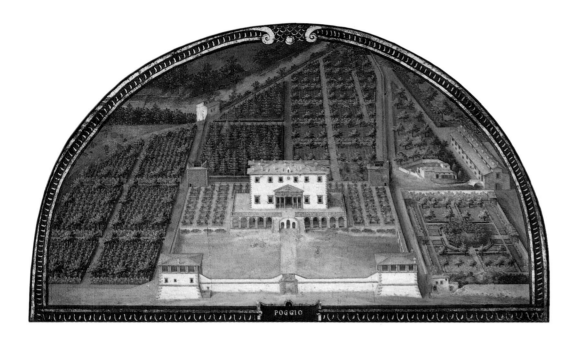

POGGIO

as the Villa's furniture; 14 of the 17 lunettes have been preserved in excellent condition and can be seen in Florence at the Topographical Museum. Relatively faithful and precise in their details, in spite of some errors, these paintings are indispensable tools for research, for they give a good idea of the estates' original aspect. Unfortunately, the depiction is somewhat deformed because Utens, attempting to include the entire estate (house, gardens, woods, buildings, roads), used an imaginary bird's-eye view in each lunette, an option which prevented him from accurately representing the perspective.

This collection of villas celebrates the Medicean heritage in the Florentine landscape and bears witness to the time when the family basked in absolute power. Artimino, Ferdinand I's favorite villa, built in 1594 by Buontalenti, was the last prestigious Medici commission and marks the end their great achievements. After 1650, their power declined. In 1737, Gian-Gastone died without descendants and the Grand Duchy of Tuscany passed first into the hands of the House of Lorraine, and then was annexed by the Austro-Hungarian Empire. In 1859, when Tuscany became part of the kingdom of Italy, King Victor Emmanuel II began transforming some of the Medicean villas and left others to deteriorate. From then on, the villas changed hands between private owners for better or for worse. The majority today belong to the Italian State, which has been able to keep them in good condition and open them up to the public.

IL TREBBIO

The Villa Il Trebbio is north of Florence, not far from San Piero a Sieve. A rocky path fringed with cypresses winds up the hill leading directly to the imposing edifice which is shielded from view by rows of trees.

In 1451, Cosimo de' Medici the Elder decided to transform this 14th-century fortress into a livable hunting-lodge and summoned Michelozzo Michelozzi to remodel the house. The architect of Cafaggiolo, the famous Medici villa nearby, did not modify the square plan, nor the watchtower, but roofed the castellated rampart-walk that surrounds the building and pierced many openings.

Immediately to the left of the entrance runs a lovely Italian-type parterre of roses forming a verdant terrace that has been maintained through the centuries. There, Cosimo kept cages for falcons that he used for hunting. The fortified walls to the left of the villa appear to date from the 12th century.

The Medici coat of arms reigns above a semi-circular arched doorway that is high enough to allow riders to enter the courtyard. On the left, the glassed-in loggia that once housed the stables has been transformed into a vestibule. On the wall, a painted escutcheon displays the coats of arms of both the Medici and Sforza families empaled on the same shield, a testimony to Catherine Sforza's marriage with Giovanni de' Medici, who was known as *Il Popolano* (the man of the people). The wedding was held in 1497, only a year before

One of the very few Tuscan
gardens
to have preserved its original
pergola, with its promise of
cooling shade.

Giovanni's death. The foolhardy widow, who had already plotted the assassination of her first two husbands, liked to spend the summer at Il Trebbio with her son Giovanni *delle Bande Nere,* when she was not defending her native city of Forli against the Borgia pope, Alexander VI or when she was not locked up in prison. After Catherine's death, her daughter-in-law, deserted by Giovanni (who had chosen the life of a *condottiere*), lived at the villa with her son, the future Cosimo I. It was in this castle, in 1537, that the young Cosimo learned of the murder of Duke Alexander and decided to seize power in Florence.

Steep stairs ascend from the courtyard to the first floor, protected by a lean-to roof resting on an elegant Tuscan column that rises from the stone parapet. The living quarters have preserved their beautiful ceilings and have been entirely restored in the style of the 14th century. Another set of stairs climbs up the tower, whose view of the surrounding hills (culminating at 1500 feet above sea level) dominates the spectacular Mugello valley. The vast neighboring forests provided game-filled hunting grounds for the Medici.

On the left, a path leads from the villa to a lawn bordered by cypress trees on a terrace contained by the outer walls overlooking the countryside. Several steps down, an attractive brick colonnade forming a pergola laden with vines has survived since the 15th century. It is easy to imagine the fervent debates held under this arbor by members of the Neo-Platonic Academy under the patronage of Cosimo the Elder. Farther down, a vegetable garden is laid out in square beds under fig and pear trees.

In 1645, the entire property was sold by Ferdinand II and then passed through many hands, including those of the Fathers of the Oratory from Florence, who kept it up until 1864, when it was put up for auction and acquired by Prince Marcantonio Borghese. Left abandoned until 1936, it was entirely restored by Dr. Scaretti and today belongs to his descendants who keep it in good shape.

The principal attraction of Il Trebbio is the exceptional condition in which it has been preserved; almost untouched since the 15th century. The present owners of the villa have successfully combined comfort, tranquillity and intimacy, conferring an extraordinary charm on this rare treasure within the walls of a stately fortress.

The intimate inner courtyard
decorated in the fashion of most
15th-century villas, with pots of
colorful flowers and a central well.

Opposite:
The vestibule, decorated with
many engravings representing Il
Trebbio, is very simply furnished.

24

CAFAGGIOLO

Cafaggiolo is situated near Villa Il Trebbio at the entrance of the verdant valley of the Mugello, nestled in between the surrounding wooded hills. The fortified villa's façade has kept its imposing aspect, a reminder of its glorious past marked by the passage of time.

In 1451, Cosimo the Elder called upon Michelozzo Michelozzi to entirely refurbish this ancient fortress in Medici territory. As it appears in Giusto Utens' lunette, the original castellated structure, dominated by a watchtower and keep, was built on a square plan around a central inner yard and two smaller courtyards; a crenellated rampart walk, resting on corbels encircles the upper story. Michelozzo remodeled this fortress into a country villa to meet the new needs of its owner. The clever architect covered the rampart walk and turrets with a roof and replaced the original loopholes with large windows overlooking the landscape.

Soon, the edifice no longer played a defensive role, but became a peaceful villa with different functions: a summer home for the Medici family, the center of an agricultural domain, and the seat of an industrial complex. The estate was surrounded by vineyards, fields and orchards that spread along the banks of the Sieve, but it also produced majolica glazed pottery in the nearby town of Cafaggiolo. At the death of Cosimo I, the property consisted of thirty farms, nine smaller buildings, many cottages, a mill, three kilns and twenty-three acres of woodlands.

The right side of the façade with its fortress-like appearance; consoles and rampart walk were made more pleasant by adding a roof and opening large windows on the ground floor.

Cafaggiolo was particularly appreciated by the Medici as a place of leisure. Cosimo I created a natural wild-animal reserve in the vast fir and pine forests behind the villa, for hunting. Francesco I often resided there in the company of his young Venetian mistress Bianca Cappello. He hunted in the forest in the same manner as his predecessor. Ferdinand I and members of the Habsburg-Lorraine family, who were to inherit the domain, continued this tradition.

Over the centuries at Cafaggiolo, a healthy outdoor life of Humanist inspiration was the rule. The overseer, who sent regular reports to Piero de' Medici on the activities of his son, made the following remarks: "Yesterday we went fishing; we caught enough fish for our dinner and returned home at a reasonable hour... Madonna Contessina [Piero's mother], Lorenzo and Giulio accompanied by servants went to visit the monks in the forest and attended high mass." The two children, future patrons of the Florentine arts were educated by Politian and often attended the debates between their tutor and his friends, Pico della Mirandola and Marsilio Ficino. This intellectual atmosphere became an inspiration for the bucolic poetry of Lorenzo the Magnificent.

The house is still bordered on the left by several long farm buildings from the former agricultural estate (stables, sharecropper cottages, barns).

In the park, a weeping willow,
planted in the 19th century,
typical of the English landscape-
style garden.

But life at Cafaggiolo went through periods of violence during the Florentine Republic's troubles. The fortress' thick walls gave refuge to the famous Lorenzino (Musset's *Lorenzaccio*) after he killed his reigning cousin, the Duke Alexander de' Medici in 1537. A few years later in 1576, at Cafaggiolo, young Eleanor of Toledo, spurned by Piero de' Medici, sought the company of other admirers and was brutally assassinated by her husband.

The atmosphere was lighter and more animated when Ferdinand I spend his falls there: "On Sunday, His Highness went hunting at Il Trebbio, then, after dinner, He gave audience to the foreigners [ambassadors, cardinals, princes], then, to amuse Madame and the Princely Children, invited all the young girls from the neighborhood and gave a ball in the field."

In 1864, the villa, along with Il Trebbio, was sold by the Italian government to Prince Marcantonio Borghese, who decided to play down its martial appearance and gave it the aspect that it has today. He tore down the keep, the battlement and the barbicans on each side of the entrance tower, thus creating a single courtyard. The moats were filled in and the drawbridges removed. The Medici coat of arms high up above the entrance was replaced by a huge clock more in keeping with the taste of the day. Inside, the whitewashed groin vaults were decorated in the latest Gothic Revival style by Leto Chini in 1887, and a colorful display of escutcheons lightened the austere atmosphere.

A witness to the tumultuous era of the rise of the Medici, Cafaggiolo remains strangely fascinating with its ascetic and military aspect, more reminiscent of medieval castles than any of the other Tuscan villas. Today Cafaggiolo is in the hands of a private company which strives to preserve this fine example of the transformations that affected the villas around Florence from the 14th century on.

CAREGGI

To the northwest of Florence, near Sesto Fiorentino, lies the town of Careggi. The Medici villa bearing the same name stands inside a vast complex of clinics and institutes belonging to the medical school, and the house itself serves as an annex to Santa Maria Nuova General Hospital. A monumental portal opens into a vast park created almost entirely in the 19th century. Visitors are admitted to the house through a door on the east side that leads into a central courtyard.

In 1417, the original 14th-century fortified castle was bought by the Medici family. In 1457, Cosimo the Elder had it entirely refurbished and enlarged by his favorite architect, Michelozzo Michelozzi. His design was entirely successful in creating a harmonious compact volume in spite of an asymmetrical plan, with the three façades (east, south and west) in perfect balance. However, the structure was modified over the centuries by several additions. Two lower lateral wings, attributed to Sangallo, were added on to the west façade towards the end of the 15th century. In the 19th century, Francis Joseph Sloane, an English aristocrat and owner of the property, built a trapezoidal-shaped extension on the north side. From this date on, the house has kept its unusual, somewhat triangular composition. The rooms bordering the irregularly-shaped inner courtyard, however, maintain a rigorously geometrical layout.

Outside, an ivy-covered wall follows the curve of the east façade, stretching south along the old road that skirted the building in the

The inner courtyard bathed
in a soft light, viewed
from the first floor.

Left:
In the background of the
16th-century cellar, the entrance
wall adorned by a small rocaille
grotto with a fountain.

Right:
Detail of the vaulted ceiling.

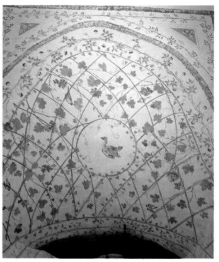

15th century. A small door provides access to a simple courtyard surrounded by an arcade with delicate columns and finely-sculpted Corinthian capitals. This idyllic spot is pervaded with a calm and studious atmosphere.

The visitor can well understand why the Medici preferred Careggi to all their other houses. Cosimo the Elder considered it to be an ideal intellectual center and adopted it for the seat of his Neo-Platonic Academy, the birthplace of Humanism. Every November 17, these historic walls reunited Marsilio Ficino, Pico della Mirandola and Politian, often accompanied by artists such as Michelozzo, Donatello, Michelangelo and Leon Battista Alberti, who all celebrated Plato's birthday in due solemnity. In this favorite retreat, Cosimo the Elder, his son Piero de' Medici and his grandson, Lorenzo the Magnificent, all spent many happy days, grateful to be able to live in such an idyllic environment.

Unfortunately the villa was stripped of its riches over the centuries; Verrocchio's famous bronze *Boy with the Dolphin,* for example, now adorns the fountain in the forecourt of the Palazzo Vecchio in Florence. Nonetheless, several pieces remain to recount the splendors of the past. The cellar's vault is entirely decorated with frescos simulating a vine-covered pergola inhabited by different kinds of birds, laughing cherubs and impudent satyrs. The floor is laid with a beautiful pavement of colored mosaics with fleur-de-lys motifs. This charming ensemble, dedicated to Bacchus, was created after 1529 when the villa was restored after being ravaged by a fire set by a republican faction called the *Arrabbiati* (the Enraged).

A doorway in the courtyard beyond the main staircase leads into the salon. Today, this room with its vaulted ceiling painted with beautiful frescos is used by the hospital administration. Cosimo I commissioned two great artists, Pontormo and Bronzino, to paint the lunettes with picturesque subjects (bucolic landscapes, other Medici villas, gardens, mythical and war scenes).

On the esplanade to the left stands an orangery with crenellated walls and greenhouses. These outbuildings enclose a small garden with parterres of boxwood and flowers lined with potted lemon and almond trees. Past the basin, to the west, two parallel wings covered with wisteria and bordered by urns with palm trees feature tall arched windows that were cut in the 19th century to obtain a better view, creating a coherent relationship between the house and the garden. A lovely loggia screened by slender columns designed by Sangallo adds lightness and grace to the top of the right wing; it is the first model of its kind and has been copied many times since the 16th century.

On the south side of the house lies the 19th-century park which nevertheless matches perfectly well Michelozzo's façade. Along the central alley paved with a mosaic of pebbles, parterres of flowers enhanced by potted lemon trees add colorful notes to the setting. Two strange statues of dwarfs, one perched on a snail, another on an owl,

Detail of a 19th-century fresco
by the English painter George
Frederick Watts in one
of the south rooms; in 1492,
having failed to save Lorenzo
the Magnificent's life, the physician
was thrown into a well
by the prince's friends.

Below:
Detail of the cellar floor.

A majestic fig tree provides shade
for the small garden adorned
by a small basin of water-lilies
in front of the crenellated
orangery.

The main garden to the south is planted with small lawns,
palms and various other kinds of trees (pine, oak, fig, cypress)
scattered here and there.

Sangallo's airy loggia, open on
three sides, attached to the
southwest corner of the house.

adorn the path that leads into the English-style garden. There, among
the trees lies a small circular basin filled with water lilies which is
encircled by several convenient ivy-covered arbors offering a choice of
shaded seats for a peaceful rest. Farther away, a fence marks the
transition between the garden and the park.

In spite of an odd assortment of structures, Careggi successfully
combines the massive and ponderous aspect of a medieval construction with the congenial surroundings typical of the Renaissance. It
presents the specific charm of a palimpsest, further amplified in the
19th century by the transformation of the garden into a English
landscape-style park.

Opposite:
The loggia's superb coffered ceiling
was decorated with grotesques
at the end of the 16th century.

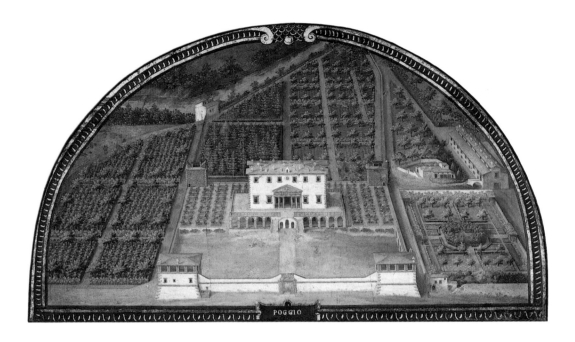

POGGIO A CAIANO

Villa Poggio a Caiano, situated to the west of Florence near Campi, in a town that bears the same name, stands on a hillock (*poggio* in Italian) offering a panorama of the Ombrone valley. An unhampered view of the grandiose façade of the house emerges through a central doorway that opens onto a broad path lined with rows of cedars of Lebanon. The original 14th-century castle belonged to the chancellors of Pistoia and was transformed in the 15th century by the Strozzi family who called it Anbra ("amber" in Italian) taken from the name of a small island in the nearby Ombrone river. After being confiscated, the property was bought back in 1490 by Lorenzo the Magnificent de' Medici, who commissioned Giuliano da Sangallo to dress it up. Constructed with two identical parallel wings flanking the central core, the building rests on an arcaded basement that forms a broad terrace at the first-floor level. From here, the panorama extends toward the towns of Florence, Prato, Pistoia and to the crests of the surrounding hills.

The pure lines of the quoins in *pietra serena* accentuate the pleasingly-proportioned façade. The red-brick arches and elegant pediment of the temple-like portico, screened by four Ionic columns and two pilasters projecting slightly from the wall, create an impression of order and harmony. Expressly commissioned by Pope Leo X, the son of Lorenzo, the portico of Greek inspiration gracefully replaces the rusticated doorways so typical of Tuscan villas. In the 18th century

Panorama of the park enclosed by walls.

Below left:
A glimpse of the right side of the villa through pine trees.

Below right:
The neoclassic façade of the orangery seen from the garden.

Below left:
The two curved stairs designed in 1807 brought
about the enlargement of the central part of the terrace
and a new series of arches.

Below right and page 42 above:
Sangallo's masterpiece: the portico's pediment decorated
with a terra cotta blue and white enamel frieze executed
by the Della Robbia family.

an elegant clock tower was added to the top of the façade emphasizing the upward thrust of the triangular pediment. The two straight ramps that rose to the terrace and could be climbed on horseback, as depicted in the lunette painted by Giusto Utens, were replaced in the early 19th century by two curvilinear stairs with double banisters.

A beautiful majolica ceiling decorates the portico that open onto a vestibule whose walls are painted with 19th-century grisailles. These frescos render a romantic homage to Lorenzo the Magnificent as "the great philanthropist." Accompanied by the Nymph Amber, he is represented offering flowers to a bust of Plato; in another scene he is shown granting approval to the maquette of the villa submitted to him by Sangallo.

The grand salon occupies the center of the edifice and flaunts a barrel-vaulted ceiling decorated with gilt and polychrome stuccos. The walls are covered with frescos begun in 1521 by Andrea del Sarto, Pontormo and Franciabigio, and completed by Alessandro Allori in 1579. These scenes depict some of the glorious events of the Roman Empire—apt symbols of the accomplishments of the Medici. *The Return of Cicero from Exile* suggests the return of Cosimo the Elder to Florence; *Consul Titus Flaminius Addressing the Achaian League* refers to the episode of the Diet of Cremona, when Lorenzo the Magnificent foiled the projects of the Venetians; *Julius Caesar Receiving Tribute from Egypt* alludes to gifts sent by the Sultan of Egypt to Lorenzo; *Syphax of Numidia Receives Scipio, Vanquisher of Hasdrubal in Spain* refers to Lorenzo's voyages to Naples. The doors are surmounted by the escutcheons of Leo X and Francesco I de' Medici, who commissioned these allegorical frescoes. The left-wall lunette houses Pontormo's masterpiece, painted in a very modernistic style, depicting Vertumnus, the god of vegetation and his wife, Pomona, along with peasants. The right-wall lunette shows *The Garden of the Hesperides,* which is attributed to Allori.

The salon opens onto a sumptuous dining hall enhanced by golden wall-coverings and a superb vaulted ceiling decorated with stucco flowers, griffins and bronze escutcheons on a white background. Painted in the 17th century by Antonio Domenico Gabbiani, the central fresco depicts the theme of *Florence Presenting Cosimo the Elder to Jupiter.*

On the same floor, the 19th-century apartments of King Victor Emmanuel II and his morganatic wife, the Countess of Mirafiori, are open to the public. Suspended stairs of a daring construction descend to the ground floor and lead to a small theater, a billiard room and various apartments. Bianca Cappello's room is adorned with a beautiful

The sumptuous salon bathed in sunlight replaced
the traditional inner courtyard in the 16th century; historical
scenes and allegorical figures were inserted in a trompe-l'œil
architectural decor under the direction of Pope Leo X.

Opposite:
The portico's superb vaulted ceiling in majolica with floral motifs designed by the Della Robbia family. On the far wall are traces of frescos painted by Filippino Lippi.

Above:
The long perspective of the ground-floor arcades enhanced by brick-red pillars.

Left:
The refinement of each detail, the pure vertical lines and the play of shadow and light are a perfect expression of the Tuscan style.

An artificial rocaille islet stands out in the center
of a basin surrounded by a low wall of stones.

chimney piece bearing two marble atlantes sculpted by Bandinelli and portraits of Bianca painted by the School of Bronzino. This is where Francesco I's adventuress found shelter from gossip and where the couple was finally united after both Francesco's wife, Joanna of Austria, and Bianca's husband died. They lived here until both of them were struck by a fever on the same day in 1587.

Through the arcades, steps provide access to the English landscape-style garden that skirts the right-hand side of the building. Lawns bordered with flowers, potted lemon and palm trees, and scattered pines have replaced the original formal Italian garden. The orangery on the left-hand side closes off the terrace overlooking the town.

Farther to the right, the garden leads into woods that once extended all the way to the Arno. These woods, filled with age-old trees (ilex, magnolia, cedar) were the favorite hunting grounds of Francesco and Bianca and have preserved their primitive look even though they are now threaded with many open and shaded paths. Hidden away on a small islet, waiting to be discovered by adventurous visitors, is a small secluded temple adorned with sculptures personifying the Ombrone river in pursuit of Amber, the nymph who was changed into an island. Lorenzo preferred this villa to all others and gave lasting fame to these mythical lovers in his poems, as did his private tutor, the Humanist and poet Politian.

Poggio a Caiano seems to have been the favorite spot of many women as well. It offered a refuge to the impetuous Bianca, who liked to organize extravaganzas; it allowed Princess Margaret Louise, the wife of Cosimo III, to hide from the scandals provoked by her infidelity and capricious behavior; it provided a stop-over to many princesses (Eleanor of Toledo, Joanna of Austria, Christine of Lorraine) on their way to Florence and gave them occasions to entertain their future husbands.

The visitor is utterly carried away by this site steeped in history. It is a perfect model of Renaissance architecture inspired by Roman antiquity and is the first Medici villa that lost its fortress-like appearance, all the while keeping its systems of defense.

View from the terrace of the English landscape-style garden.

CASTELLO

Villa Castello stands on a small rise, not far from Careggi, in a region northwest of Florence. The original castle was a 13th-century fortress built around an inner courtyard with a covered colonnade. In 1477, it was bought and transformed by the Medici, but, because of its strategic value, it was fought over and ravaged by opposing factions in 1527 during the family's exile from Florence. In 1538, the newly-appointed Duke Cosimo I de' Medici, victor at the battle of Montemurlo, decided to settle there to enjoy the tranquillity of the site. He commissioned the architect Niccolo Tribolo to entirely redesign the estate. Cosimo lived there with his second wife, Camilla Martelli, until his death in 1574. The property remained in the family until the middle of the 18th century and was then passed on to the House of Lorraine. Several further transformations took place, especially under the auspices of the Grand Duke Pietro Leopoldo, who had many frescos executed. It was acquired by the State in 1924.

The simple, broad white façade bordered by a rather arid lawn seems designed to discourage visitors, for the lovely rusticated entrance designed by Buontalenti remains obstinately closed and visits are not permitted within. However, this first impression soon changes upon entering the gates to the right of the building. From the lawn skirting the rear façade, the view of the vast expanse of the formal Italian gardens that gradually rise up the slopes of Mount Morello, terrace by terrace, until they reach the woods beyond, is a

Opposite:
The façade of the castle, seat
of the Accademia della Crusca
since 1974.

Above:
Lunette painted by Giusto Utens,
1598, Topographical Museum,
Florence: the fabulous garden
layout created by Tribolo;
from front to back, the fish pools,
the castle flanked by its two small
secret gardens; to the West,
the Hercules and Antaeus fountain;
in the center, the fountain of
Venus inside a maze, a first wall
that no longer exists, a second wall
housing the animal grotto, the
woods and the Basin of Apennines.

View of the north façade, the Italian parterres, masterpiece
of Tribolo's project, and the fountain of Hercules and Antaeus.
In the foreground a star motif marks the erstwhile location
of the Venus fountain.

breathtaking marvel of perspective sequences.

Tribolo, a man of many talents (sculptor, engineer, topographer, hydrologist), laid out the main gardens in a harmonious geometrical plan on either side of a north-south axis linking the Arno to Mount Morello, as shown in Giusto Utens' lunette. On the east and west sides of the house, he added small secret gardens filled with flowers and aromatic plants (they have since disappeared). On the south side of the esplanade in front of the entrance, there were two ornamental fishponds. From this point on, an avenue of mulberry trees forming a pergola ran toward the Arno.

Extending northward, the main gardens enclosed within walls are punctuated by square parterres of boxwood planted in symmetrical patterns and highlighted by urns of flowers and potted lemon trees. In the center, stands a white octagonal fountain sculpted by Tribolo. The claws of eight griffins cling to the lower part of the shaft; four joyful cherubs hug the necks of swans spurting water from their beaks to fill the lower basin. From the second level hang four hideous billy-goat heads, above which perch four more cherubs who survey the garden with a mischievous air. A group sculpture presently under restoration depicting Hercules and Antaeus crowns the monumental fountain.

Farther up, a central path bordered by rectangular lawns and potted lemon trees leads to another part of the garden closed off on the left by an orangery and on the right by a lemon house. Here, the fountain of Venus Anadyomene, sculpted by Giambologna originally stood, but it was necessary to wander through an elaborate maze of thick cypress, bay and myrtle hedges to reach it. This fountain was transferred from Castello to the Medici villa, La Petraia, in the 18th century.

A wall marks the end of the garden. Beyond this, a well-preserved grotto set along the central axis attracts attention. A curious arch fashioned out of mosaics, seashells and sponges emerges from the shadows. Inside, three niches present sculptures of fantastic anthropomorphic animals carved out of various colored stones; the eyes of these creatures seem to follow the intruder insistently.

Outside the grotto the sunlight seems so harsh that is a relief to find shade again beneath the wall. On the right, an opening and several steps show the way towards the woods, and a winding path through the trees leads to a large basin from which rises a colossal bronze figure of an old, bent and bearded man. This figure is said to symbolize the Apennine Mountains (or Winter, according to others). Hugging himself as if shivering with cold and with a somewhat perplexed, yet irate look, he seems to be asking: "But how in the devil did you find your way here?"

The water for the different fountains and basins in Villa Castello's gardens circulates through a system of complex pipe work devised in 1537 by Piero da San Casciano, an expert hydrologist. The network

The astonishing statue
of the Apennines, sculpted in 1565
by Ammanati, jumps out
of the rock like an abominable
jack-in-the-box.

Right:
The Niche of the Bear:
in the animal grotto, sculpted
by Giambologna and his assistants
between 1565 and 1569; all the
animals of the Creation seem
to be waiting patiently for another
God, symbolized by Cosimo I,
to restore the Lost Paradise
of Eden.

was completed after his death in 1541 by Tribolo. Flowing from the Castellina Hills and from Villa La Petraia above, the water follows the incline proceeding along an aqueduct before being distributed throughout the garden.

The impression of being able to wander around at will is misleading, for, in fact, an itinerary dotted with allegories and myths was rigorously laid out by Cosimo I and further elaborated by the writer Benedetto Varchi in 1543. Each decorative element was fashioned to evoke the power of the Medici and to recall Florence's return to a Golden Age thanks to the reign of Cosimo I. This theme was developed notably in the grotto; according to legend, the purifying figure of a unicorn plunged its horn in a poisoned watering place, making it safe for the other animals to drink. Cosimo I, symbolized by the unicorn, intended to create a new earthly paradise where the Florentines could all be united under his protection. The representation of Spring as the Forces of Nature that surround Venus rising from the sea is a predominant theme of this garden (as well as the symbol of Florence) and was inspired by Botticelli's two famous paintings, *The Triumph of Spring* and *The Birth of Venus,* which were transferred to the villa at that time.

Tribolo, overwhelmed by the Duke's other commissions, never found the time to carry out his fabulous project. Completed by Buontalenti from 1550 until 1574, it underwent certain modifications.

The Castello gardens were created to glorify the reign of the Medici. Although somewhat altered, they remain a rare example of scenic imagination, the first of their kind in Europe. They aroused enthusiasm and were often copied until the 18th century.

Above:
The Demidoffs' residence (1872) abandoned
and closed to the public today.
In 1969, Prince Paul of Yugoslavia
auctioned off the last art objects.

Right:
Lunette painted by Giusto Utens, 1598, Topographical
Museum, Florence: Francesco I de' Medici's villa at the time of
its splendor and the Park of the Moderns, on the south slope
of the hillside down to the Washerwoman's Basin.

PRATOLINO

The vast domain of the former Medicean Villa Pratolino, now known as the Demidoff Park, lies to the North of Florence. The magnificent gardens, with the fountains and water courses that once aroused such rapture, have practically disappeared. But with a little imagination the splendors of the Medici reign can be brought back to life by strolling through the winding paths among the age-old trees, discovering the vestiges of a fountain here, a statue or grotto there. Built on a prince's whim as a place of pleasure, Pratolino has had a chaotic history, in turn, falling almost into oblivion and coming back to life.

Francesco I de' Medici, looking for a place to carry on his illicit love affair with Bianca Cappello, began to acquire the acreage from the Uguccioni family immediately after his marriage to Joanna of Austria in 1565. The estate as a whole was not consolidated until 1586, however, at which time it counted 50 acres of woods and more than 1400 acres of fertile land surrounding farm buildings built by Buontalenti himself. Francesco, a practitioner of alchemy, given to introspection and a strong desire to uncover Nature's secrets, intended to transform Pratolino into a place providing recreation and entertainment, replete with allegory and magic. Breaking with the traditional symmetrical design of the Tuscan garden, Pratolino was laid out as a large landscaped track of woods in which "artificial nature" was the rule and where visitors could wander as they saw fit. Many artists including

The park, one of the Florentines' favorite promenades.

Above:
The *fagianeria*, formerly Ferdinand I's carriage house, transformed into a building to raise pheasants for shooting.

Middle:
Small fountain behind the *osteria*, or inn, used to accommodate the Grand Duke's guests.

The Demidoff residence and romantic English-style garden: the landscape architect Joseph Frietsch transformed the space into lawns with scattered trees, among which he placed the sculptures.

The aviary created as a living museum to house all species of birds.

Above:
The neoclassic Montili pavilion (1820) used by the Demidoffs as a gazebo, hunting lodge and fencing room.

Middle:
Reproduction of the monument to Nicola Demidoff. The original stands in the Florentine square of that name.

The charming chapel designed by Buontalenti
behind lofty trees.

Buontalenti, Giambologna, Ammanati, Bandinelli, Francini were invited to execute statues, fountains and grottos.

Buontalenti built the house between 1570 and 1575 in the center of the property as well as many of the other buildings that are scattered throughout the park: the *paggeria* (the house of pages, buffoons and dwarfs), an inn and hotel (for the guests), stables and a flour mill. Designed on the same model as Poggio a Caiano, the house was constructed on a base of solid walls pierced with many grottos filled with automatons. These were run by hydraulic bellows, a system much admired by Montaigne, who visited Pratolino in 1580: "Not only is the music and harmony activated hydraulically, but several statues are water-driven, the animals bend down to drink and there are many other concealed mechanisms. In a minute, the whole grotto fills with water, and the seats get your bottom wet." In 1579, the villa, then beautifully furnished, was finally ready to receive Francesco and Bianca Cappello's guests for their wedding; the couple began to spend long periods there in each others company.

When they both died eight years later, Ferdinand I de' Medici employed various artists to continue the project, including Mechini, Giulio and Alfonso Parigi, Ferdinando Tacca, Antonio Ferri and Alessandro Galilei. The house's walls were redecorated with baroque frescos and hung with a beautiful collection of 17th-century paintings. On the third floor, a theater was built for lyric performances. The Grand Duke held court at Pratolino, and princes, ambassadors and prestigious travelers filed through the villa, which had become a crossroads and a model throughout Europe. Many found inspiration in the architecture and decoration; the technology of the automatons was copied; the fountains and statues were often imitated.

The advent of the House of Lorraine put an end to the splendors of Pratolino. The 18th-century mentality had become too far removed from that of the preceding centuries. In 1779, Pietro Leopoldo, who considered the villa to be a useless luxury, began to rid it of its most precious belongings: the collection of paintings (more than 150 canvases), the sculptures, theater sets, furniture and tapestries were transferred to the Palazzo Pitti; the fountains were taken apart and their statues placed in the Boboli Gardens; the woods became hunting grounds; the farm buildings and land were sold, and the annexes turned into factories. The water used for the fountains was deviated to provide for industry and the empty house began to be eaten away at its foundations by water infiltration. The destruction of the building accelerated during the Napoleonic era and the woods were left in a sad state of abandon.

In 1818, Ferdinand III of Lorraine took pity on Pratolino and decided to bring it back to life, but in another form. Joseph Frietsch, a Bohemian landscape architect, was commissioned to transform the woods into a romantic English-style park, increasing the size from 50 to 190 acres. The old Medici house, undermined by leakage, was torn

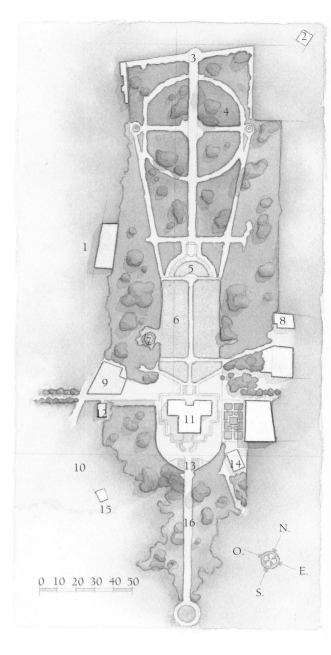

Layout of Pratolino's grounds in the 16th century taken from J.C. Shepherd and G.A. Jellicoe, *Italian Gardens of the Renaissance*, London 1986:

1) Park of the Ancients, 2) Montili Pavilion, 3) Fountain of Jupiter, 4) Labyrinth of Bay Trees, 5) Basin of Appenines, 6) Alley of the Great Men, 7) Chapel, 8) Demidoff Residence, 9) Osteria or inn, 10) Park of the Moderns, 11) Medici House, 12) Mask Pond, 13) Mugnone Grotto, 14) Aviary, 15) Fagianeria, 16) Alley of Dancing Water, 17) Washerwoman's Basin.

down. In 1872, Prince Paolo Demidoff, a rich businessman of Russian origin who had settled in Florence in 1824, bought the property. Demidoff continued the refurbishing; he completed the enclosing wall, opened up alleys, restored statues and turned the old *paggeria* into his own residence, furnishing it and decorating it with great luxury. Pratolino, however, was ravaged once again after the death of the last of the Demidoffs. In 1981, the Province of Florence purchased the estate and since then has made an effort to return it to its former splendor.

The Medici woods that spread over the whole hillside forming the Pratolino estate were separated at the summit by a wall dividing them into two distinct areas: the Park of the Ancients on the north side and the Park of the Moderns on the south. This sloping terrain was adorned by a superb alley called the Promenade of Fountains. These were fed by water streaming forth from the Fountain of Jupiter, crossing a maze of bay trees, filling the Basin of Apennines, flowing through the Field of the Great Men that displayed twenty-six antique-style statues, dipping under the villa, to resurface on the south slope, then ducking into the Grotto of Mugnone, rushing out again into to the Alley of Dancing Water and ending its course in the Washer-woman's Basin.

Today, most of these elements have disappeared and it is no longer possible to follow the original water works along the north-south axis. The Demidoff residence has unfortunately been deprived of its interior riches and is not open to visitors; neither are the other extant buildings. However, the charming chapel built in 1580 from a design by Buontalenti is in good repair; this hexagonal edifice is surmounted by a lanterned dome and surrounded by a small portico, a structure that permitted servants to attend Mass from outside the building.

Giambologna's famous statue representing Apennines has also been well preserved. Looming out from a mass of trees, a terrifying colossus covered with bristling hair and beard, his body dripping with pieces of rocaille, holds down with his left hand the gushing head of a monster lying at his feet. This gigantic prehistoric-type creature is perched on a rocky island that used to be surrounded by a small basin; a larger, more romantic pond was added in the 19th century.

The Mugnone Fountain, with its niche of rustic rocaille, boasts a representation of the river god sculpted by Giambologna in 1577; the Mask Pond, although damaged, still exposes a dreadful giant whose contorted face contemplates the water.

Pratolino is a unique 16th-century example of a fantastic park created and brought to life by a poetic spirit as an homage to the forces of Nature. The poor state of preservation, the scars of time, the dismantling and the multiple transformations notwithstanding the evocative power of this fabulous garden's vestiges exert a singular fascination and trigger the imagination.

Foot of Apennines statue.
In the 19th century the feet
and hands were replaced;
the originals now lie in front
of the Demidoff residence.

Left:
The imposing giant representing
Apennines, approximately 30 ft.
high, sculpted by Giambologna
in 1579-80; above the islet behind
the sculpture, were several grottos
painted with frescos and filled
with automatons and fountains;
these no longer exist.

Above:
The south façade of La Petraia; the central alley leads up
through the Italian-style parterres to a fountain recessed under
the double staircase. Two levels higher, the entrance door is
surmounted by the escutcheon of the Medici and Lorraine
families; above, the clock tower crowns the edifice.

Right:
Lunette painted by Giusto Utens, 1598, Topographical
Museum, Florence; in the foreground, the Italian-style
parterres, then the fishpond and farther back the terrace
in front of the villa with more parterres on the right, replaced
by the Garden of the Figurine in the 18th century.

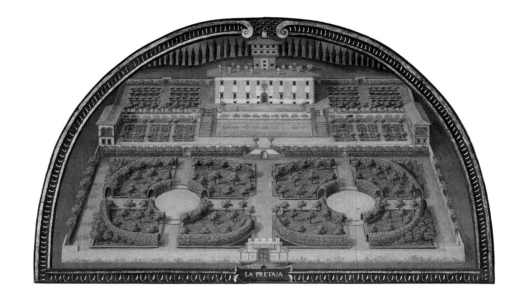

La Petraia

La Petraia is situated to the northwest of Florence near Villa Castello. The ancient 13th-century *casa da signore* belonging to the Brunelleschi family was taken over by the Strozzi in the 15th century and then, in 1530, confiscated by the Medici. In 1568, Cosimo I gave it to his son Ferdinand, who commissioned Buontalenti, in 1591, to transform it into a comfortable residence. The architect preserved the square plan of the medieval edifice constructed around a courtyard. The harmonious façade cut with generous windows is dominated by a 14th-century watch tower resting on molded corbels, giving the ensemble a fortress-like appearance despite the additions of a clock and mullioned windows in the 16th century. Buontalenti also renovated the sloping garden which kept its layout until the 18th century.

Past the outbuildings to the right, a portal cut in the surrounding wall gives access to the garden. A broad alley leads to a clearing surrounded by bushes and trees forming a delightful shady spot in front of an arrangement of Italian-style parterres. Directly beyond, up several steps leading to a small mound rimmed with circular hedges and adorned by a simple three-tiered fountain, the vast prospect of the garden rising up to the house, terrace by terrace, spreads out before the eye.

Past this fountain added in the 18th century, the walk surrounded by intricate parterres of topiary, white flowers and bordered by potted lemon and pear trees, a double staircase ascends to an intermediary level featuring a large fish pond in the center, parterres of boxwood and flowers on the left and, to the right, a small garden planted with palm trees in the 19th century. A straight flight of steps with wrought-iron banisters provides access to the terrace on which the house stands.

On this level, the Figurine Garden, named after the central fountain, once held the bronze statue of Venus—symbol of Florence—executed by Giambologna for the Castello gardens. This piece, decorated with sea gods astride dolphins, cherubs, fauns and masks, is under restoration at the moment. A reproduction of the statue of Venus, absentmindedly wringing out her long hair between her fingers, can be seen in the *studiolo*. An elegant cast-iron and cement belvedere adds a finishing touch at the south east corner of the terrace. This little building was erected at the end of the 19th century and contains a small vestibule and an octagonal room with huge windows and a heavy stucco decor. The terrace, planted today with hedged-trimmed lawns, was originally an Italian-style garden with parterres and espaliers of citrus fruit growing on the walls. Cypress trees rise up behind the Figurine Garden. These woods are open to the public with access through a door farther along the wall. Between 1836 and 1850, a Bohemian landscape architect, Joseph Frietsch, designed this romantic park with paths winding among the various species of trees and over small bridges spanning streams.

Inside the house, an entrance hall opens directly onto a grand colorful ballroom. The decoration of what used to be the central courtyard began at the time of Ferdinand I, when his new wife, Christine of Lorraine, commissioned Cosimo Daddi—most likely assisted by the young Cigoli—to paint frescos on the north and south walls. Surmounted by a row of escutcheons of the Medici-Lorraine families, these are entirely adorned by grotesques and historic scenes. Set in frames, they represent the Siege of Jerusalem by Godefroy de Bouillon, the first hero of the Lorraine dynasty.

When Cosimo II took over the estate in 1609 he commissioned paintings from many artists and built up a sizable collection. Some of them were hung temporarily on the walls of the east-west double loggia as a reminder of the picture gallery of the Athenian Propylae. According to Baldinucci's, account: "There was such a strong wind that, in no time, many of the oil paintings had fallen down... So that this would not happen again, his Highness decided to decorate the courtyard with frescos." Starting in 1636, the young artist Volterrano spent twelve years depicting the *Splendor of the Medici House* in a highly colored Baroque style without following the historic chronology of the events.

In 1865, when Florence was named capital of the Kingdom of Italy, the property became the private residence of King Victor Emmanuel II and underwent many transformations to make it worthy of a monarch's palace. The courtyard, never enclosed before, was turned into a

Above:
The former inner courtyard transformed
into a ballroom in the 19th century, lit by the sun
through the glass roof.

Right:
The flamboyant dining room draped in red silk and furnished
in pure 19th-century fashion with Flemish School tapestries
dating from the 18th century.

ballroom surmounted with a glass roof and the floor enlaid with a star-patterned mosaic.

Through the east portal lies the little chapel entirely decorated with frescos painted by Pier Dandini between 1682 and 1695; the daring vault depicts, with typically Baroque verve, different figures surrounding the Virgin. On the first floor, to the left of the chapel, are the private apartments of Victor Emmanuel II and his morganatic wife, Countess Mirafiori, which include a game room with a large collection of parlor games and billiard and roulette tables.

In 1919, the property was bought by the Italian State and opened to the public. La Petraia remains a typical example of a 16th-century villa, rebuilt on a medieval structure that underwent many changes over the centuries. In spite of these modifications, however, the villa has retained all of its beauty.

Above:
Halfway up the Viale del Poggio Imperiale on a spectacular
north perspective lies the impressive beige and ivory
neoclassic façade of Poggio Imperiale.

Right:
Anonymous, after Alfonso Parigi, *Jousting at Poggio Imperiale,
in honor of Prince Ladislas of Poland*, 1624, Topographical
Museum, Florence: the north façade built by Parigi, adorned
by many Baroque marble statues.

POGGIO IMPERIALE

From Florence's south entrance, the Porta Romana, the Viale del Poggio Imperiale ascends the hillside to a villa bearing the same name. The road leads directly into a semi-circular clearing in front of the residence where jousting and feasts were held in the 17th century.

Looking at the stately neoclassic façade with its majestic proportions it is no longer possible to recognize the ancient 15th-century *casa da signore* originally called Poggio Baroncelli after the family that had it built. In 1565, Cosimo I gave it to his favorite daughter, Isabella, and to her husband, Paolo Giordano Orsini, Duke of Bracciano. The new owner did nothing to change the structure of the building but simply adorned it with family portraits and statues. After his death in 1576, the Orsini family, having retained their rights to the villa, sold it in 1622 to Mary Magdalene of Austria, widow of Cosimo II.

The Grand Duchess decided to refurbish and enlarge it, giving it the name of Poggio Imperiale to evoke her family ties to the reigning house of Austria. Giulio Parigi won the architectural contest that she had organized and finished the reconstruction in two years. He designed an elegant three-storied façade crowned with a triple-arch belvedere, lengthened on both sides by two wings followed by a circular balustrade enclosing a vast exedra in front of the villa.

Several steps lead up to the main entrance of the building and give access to the arcades with arched windows that surround the central courtyard. The wings on each side were designed by Giulio

Sunlit arcade surrounding the central courtyard, almost in its original state, built by Parigi in the 18th century.

Right:
18th-century plan of Poggio Imperiale, in G. Ruggieri, *Piante dei palazzi, ville e giardini del Granducate di Toscana*, Florence, 1742; the Parigi wings (early 17th century) extending from both sides of the central courtyard to the east and the west, and to the south the Marmi wing (late 17th century).

Parigi and have been preserved. On the ground floor of the right wing, five rooms—the former apartments of Mary Magdalene of Austria and her son Ferdinand II—still bear their original decoration, of which the magnificent formal audience room is the best example. The Grand Duchess and her mother-in-law, Christine of Lorraine, who acted as regents during Ferdinand II's childhood, hunted on the estate and organized sumptuous festivities and banquets.

In 1631, at Mary Magdalene's death, her eldest son and his wife, Vittoria della Rovere, inherited Poggio Imperiale. With a particular taste for the splendor of the Baroque style, she had the architect Giacinto Marmi add a third wing to the south of the central courtyard between 1681 and 1683, and considerably increased the collections of art objects and paintings from the 16th and 17th centuries that have since been transferred to the Pitti and Uffizi Galleries. Abandoned for a time by the Lorraine family, which had inherited the property, the villa found a new period of magnificence under Pietro Leopoldo. In 1766, Leopoldo, who had decided to make Poggio Imperiale his main residence, commissioned the architect Gaspero Paoletti to give it an even more grandiose aspect in harmony with the taste of the times.

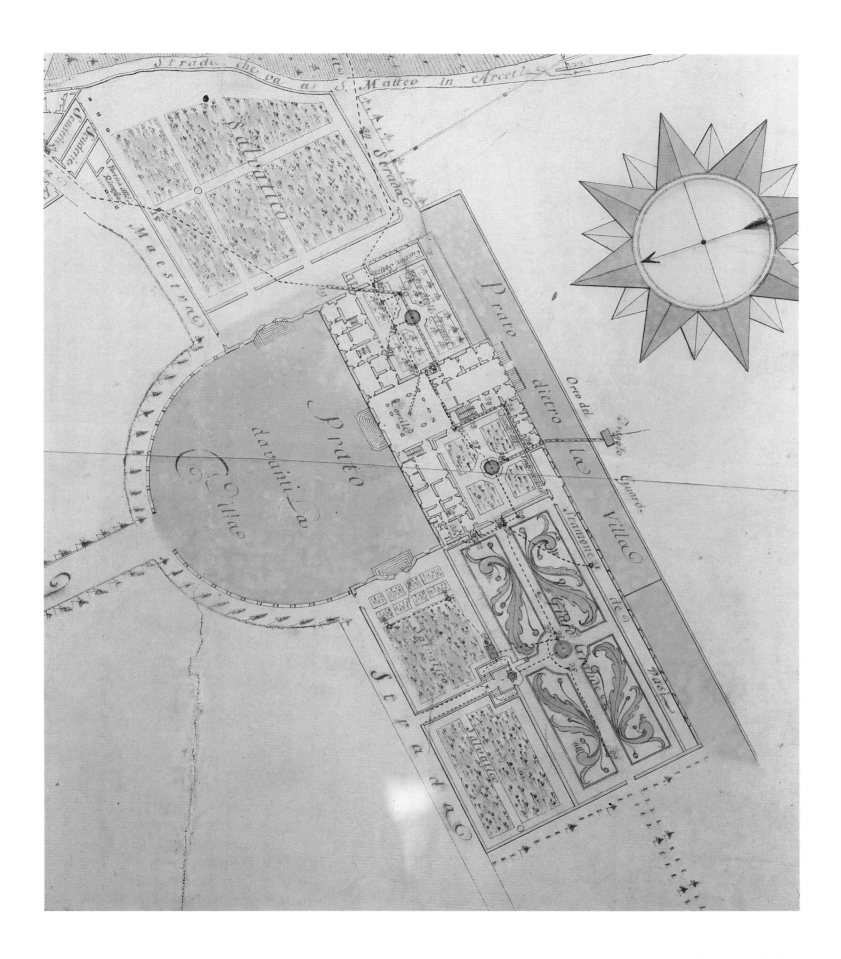

Above:
The majestic neoclassic façade built in two stages; the
engaged, four-columned portico with its pediment by Cacialli
in 1809, set above the rusticated ground-floor arcade designed
by Poccianti in 1806. The inscription states that the villa has
been a private girls' school since 1865.

Paoletti was able to integrate the Florentine traditions of the Renaissance while at the same time adapting the classicist demands of the 18th century. The transformations continued until 1782. The Grand Duke spent more on this project alone than for the combined restoration of three other villas: Poggio a Caiano, Castello and La Petraia.

Paoletti doubled the size of the building by attaching two perpendicular additions to the south end on either side of the Marmi wing. Then he joined these, on the north end, onto the two Parigi wings by affixing new rooms on the east and west sides. The building had by now taken on a rectangular plan which included three inner courtyards. The two lateral ones enclosed secret gardens designed in the 17th century; the one to the east was planted with flower beds; in the other was an orange grove. They have since been transformed into simple lawns.

The architect's rigorous treatment of all the façades established a logical relationship between the different architectural elements. The east-west courtyards are articulated vertically by an alternation of large windows crowned with triangular or semi-circular pediments and twin Tuscan pilasters on the ground floor and Ionic pilasters on the first floor. Horizontal cornices clearly mark the level of each story. In front of the west façade, the original boxwood parterre laid out in the 17th century remains with its central fountain and small woods beyond.

In order to match the frescoed rooms of earlier periods and preserve a sense of continuity throughout the building, Pietro Leopoldo commissioned several Tuscan painters, among whom Tommaso Gherardini, Giuliano Traballesi and Giuseppe Fabbrini, to decorate the new ground-floor rooms on the south and west wings in the neoclassic style that was then very much in vogue. The apartments on the first floor were covered with white stucco against a pastel background and adorned with romantic and mythological scenes above the doors and Venetian mirrors. Oriental silk and Chinese wallpaper covered the walls.

In 1806, one year before her deposition, the Queen of Etruria, Marie Louise of Bourbon, gave orders to Pasquale Poccianti to refurbish the façade entirely. The architect only had time enough to raise the front colonnade. Another architect, Giuseppe Cacialli, took over this project several years later under the orders of the new Grand Duchess, Elisa Baciocchi, sister of Napoleon I. He built a story above the arcades and crowned it with a pediment adorned by a large clock held by two antique Victories in bas-relief. In 1814, under the reign of Ferdinand III of Habsburg, the work on the façade was finally completed with the construction of two projecting additions: to the right, the guard-house and to the left, a chapel. The final result can only be qualified as acceptably academic, but the large central windows do allow a great quantity of light into the gallery.

Many statues used to crown Parigi's villa in the 17th century; of these, only those of Jupiter brandishing a lightning bolt and Hercules carrying the world, placed on high pedestals on either side of the entrance way, remain today.

Opposite below left:
The ornamented wagon roof of the arcade designed by Poccianti (1806); ramps at either end allowed access on horseback.

Opposite below right:
The firm articulation of the Classical orders in the left-hand courtyard, designed by Paoletti (1768-1771); small elegant balconies underline the refined aspect of the ensemble.

The reception room painted with frescos by Matteo Rosselli
in 1623; the superb vaulted ceiling adorned with grotesques
and historic scenes; the walls hung with representations
of Medicean villas, in which Mary-Magdelene of Austria
and Christine of Lorraine received ambassadors
and foreign princes.

Ferdinand II's antechamber;
one of the five 17th-century
grand-ducal apartments that have
preserved their original frescos.

Because of its choice location on a hillside near Palazzo Pitti, Poggio Imperiale was appreciated as much by the Medici wives in the 16th and 17th century as by the grand duchesses of Tuscany in the 18th and 19th centuries. It is for this reason that the building was continually transformed throughout each of these periods. However, these changes have bestowed upon Poggio Imperiale the grand air of a palace, richly decorated, with proportions comparable to Palazzo Pitti, and it remains in excellent condition.

In the 16th century, the Republic of Florence extended much farther than the immediate outskirts of the city. It spread to the north beyond Pistoia, to the east beyond Arezzo, to the south almost to Siena and to the west as far as the Tyrrhenian Sea. The selection of villas in this book takes into account the immensity of the territory as well as the diversity of the landscape and the geographical situation of each.

Most of the Tuscan villas, such as Il Riposo dei Vescovi, La Pietra and Gamberaia, today scattered over the hillsides around Florence, existed already in the 14th century at the height of the Republic. Several, like Villoresi, date back to the 12th or 13th century. But it is almost impossible to find a Florentine villa that has kept its original medieval structure, when it was only a simple *casa da signore*. Many were torn down by the Pontifical and Imperial armies during the siege of Florence in 1530. They were often reconstructed and enlarged afterwards, thanks to the prosperity of the Grand Duchy under the rule of the Medici, who set the example themselves by refurbishing their own villas. Some, like Villoresi, have kept their Renaissance appearance. Others were not renovated until the 17th century under the stimulus of the Baroque period, for example: Celle, Ginori-Lisci and Gamberaia. Some owners preferred to commission great Roman artists such as Bernini or Carlo Fontana who redesigned the plans for Rospigliosi and La Pietra. The walls of Villoresi were covered with Empire-style frescos, the woods of Celle were transformed into a romantic park, and the Italian-style parterre of Ginori-Lisci into an English lawn, while extravagant architectural features were added to Il Riposo dei Vescovi. In the 19th century, Florence, more than any of the other Tuscan cities, became a favorite spot for foreign art amateurs, many of whom bought villas. Today most of these properties are in private hands. In order to survive, some villas have been committed to specific uses: Celle has been transformed into an institution devoted to contemporary art, I Tatti into an Art History research center, Villoresi into a luxurious hotel and restaurant, Rospigliosi into a center for receptions and conventions. None belong to the State, but most are accessible to visitors who manifest a true interest in Florentine art.

In spite of their successive transformations, many of the Florentine villas retain a plain and almost severe aspect which is particularly apparent in the most famous examples: La Pietra and Gamberaia. The simple charm, and human touch, the intimacy and serenity that emanate from these villas sets them apart from those of Lucca or Sienna.

The front façade of Villa La Pietra.

VILLORESI

Villoresi is an ancient villa with a surprising history. It stands in the small town of Sesto Fiorentino to the northwest of Florence.

Lost in the countryside, this ancient fortress was planned with two lateral wings around a central courtyard surmounted by a high tower erected in 1100 by the Della Tosa family, who were influential supporters of the pope. It became a Guelf refuge during the civil wars that divided Florence at that time. When the Della Tosas were not at war, they were active in the wool industry. The esplanade in front of the fortress was especially reserved for sheep shearing. Only a small flower-filled central courtyard containing a well, the lower part of the tower and the surrounding rooms remain from that period. It is said that Dante's wife, Gemma Donati, took refuge in this fortress when her husband was exiled from Florence.

In 1579, when events calmed, the edifice was transformed into a residence. The walls were enlarged to allow for a 120-foot addition. On the ground floor, a large unpaved entrance gallery made it possible to enter on horseback and on the first floor, a long loggia was built from which a stunning view of the enclosed garden unfolds. Accessible from the entrance arcades, this garden was laid out in the 17th century. It has kept its boxwood parterres planted with roses and bordered by lemon and orange trees, oleanders and geraniums, as well as the outbuildings surrounded by fig and olive groves. The villa has retained the same appearance since the Renaissance although it has

The inner courtyard has preserved all its medieval charm; the first-floor corridor supported by corbels joins the two wings together; in time of war, it was used as a passageway for soldiers.

Left:
The 12th-century inner courtyard was the core of the building; the tower was partially knocked down on two occasions, once during the devastation by the Ghibelline faction in 1260 and again by the Pisans in 1364.

The pietra serena cornices, the windows and wrought-iron balconies on the first floor date from the 17th century; in the 19th century, the Villoresi family affixed their coat of arms to the façade.

The rear façade with its loggia,
said to be "the longest in Tuscany,"
seen from the delightful Italian-
style parterre; this corner
of paradise has hardly changed
since the 16th century.

passed through many hands. The Manieri and Capponi families, who lived there in the 17th century, enriched the property with a chapel that houses an altarpiece by Maso da San Frediano, a 16th-century painter. Then the Collini and Fratellesi families took the villa over in the 18th century and filled the house with the furnishings that may still be seen today.

In the beginning of the 19th century, the Villoresi, an old family of Tuscan and Savoyard origins, bought the villa as a summer residence. They successfully created a tasteful interior by adding a series of pastel-toned frescos and by having the entrance gallery paved and painted from floor to ceiling in trompe-l'œil by Alfredo Luzi in the Egyptian taste which was still in vogue at the end of the Empire. These frescos depict a balustrade surmounted with pots of flowers and antique statues running down the length of a wall underneath a mock pergola open to a blue sky with imaginary birds in flight. In the background, there is a joyous composition of pyramids, Roman sepulchers, cypress and palm trees.

On the first floor, in the rooms off the loggia, Paolo Sarti painted mythological scenes on the ceiling vaults and trompe-l'œil landscapes filled with statues, balconies, plants and flowers. In the reading-room, Bartolomeo Pinelli, who stayed at the villa for some time, offered naive pastoral scenes (peasant dances, marionette shows) to the Villoresi family in exchange for their hospitality.

During the Second World War, the Valloresi family moved into their villa on a permanent basis. In 1963, in order to maintain their patrimony, they transformed it into a hotel-restaurant. Fortunately, they had the good taste to make only minor changes. To the left of the unmodified gallery lies the corridor leading to the ground-floor rooms decorated with reproductions of 16th-century drawings or contempo-

Detail of the parterre
from the first-floor loggia; exuding
the perfumes of colorful lemon
and orange trees, oleanders,
geraniums, fig and olive trees;
an ideal spot for contemplation.

rary paintings. A little farther away is a library full of old leatherbound books. Next, the grand reception room with its groin-vaulted ceiling is adorned with painted garlands and wall coverings in trompel'œil; its walls are hung with portraits of the Medici and Lorraine families and the Villoresi genealogical tree surmounted by their coat of arms. The last three rooms comprise the original core of the 12th-century fortress and give access to the inner courtyard now given over to the hotel dining service and furnished in an overly-modern style.

Beyond the reception hall, a straight staircase leads to the loggia which houses a few pieces of wickerwork. The frescoed rooms are the hotel's most beautiful guest rooms and each has been given a small tiled bathroom. The old interior garden visible from the loggia has been removed for practical reasons and now the spot holds a swimming pool and parasols. Behind the fig and olive grove there is a secret hideaway in which an astonishing fresco *à la sepia* is tucked away. It represents a panoramic view of 15th-century Florence, a souvenir of a talented client-*cum*-artist of the hotel.

The grand gallery paved and painted with 19th-century frescos by Alfredo Luzi in the Egyptian taste still in vogue at the end of the Empire period. The Villoresi family has kept the intimate and warm character by adding potted plants, family photos, and soft lighting in all the rooms.

The trompe-l'œil decoration enhanced by mythological
statues, one of the most charming guest-rooms off the loggia.

Above:
The olive grove and the rear façade of the villa enhanced by the lovely series of arched windows underlined by an engaged balustrade.

Right
The front terrace planted with a rose parterre and scattered with several palm trees provides a touch of the exotic; the rear façade and the greenhouses on the right.

GINORI-LISCI

Villa Ginori-Lisci stands on one of Mount Acuto's foothills, not far from Villa Villoresi, in the village of Diocca. Until 1965, the famous porcelain factory, founded in 1735 by Marquis Carlo Ginori, was still in operation; it has since been transferred to Sesto.

The Ginori-Lisci family arrived in Doccia a number of centuries ago. This old Florentine family of wool and silk merchants made a considerable fortune in the 15th century through its banking operations in Naples, trading with the Orient and holding privileged relations with the Royal House of Aragon. After building the family palace in the street bearing their name in Florence, the Ginori-Lisci bought this estate with its *casa da signore* in 1525. It wasn't until 1620, however, that the owners gave in to the vogue of refurbishing villas and Lionardo di Bartolomeo transformed the simple *casa* into the splendid house that may still be seen today.

A monumental portal gives access to a lawn planted with trees leading up to yet another gateway. The alley that runs along the right side of the villa skirts a small pond adorned in the center with a rocky islet covered with moss. This water once supplied the villa and the porcelain factory. A few steps lead up to the level of the house.

The three-story main block with a wing built at a right angle is

The English-style garden dotted with lemon trees,
the greenhouses on either side and the woods of Mount Acuto
in the background; in the 17th century, the present lawn
was a small enclosed garden for medicinal plants.

Right:
The ivy-laden orangery whose
large arched windows soak up
the sun at the end of a summer
afternoon; hidden on the left
is a charming rocaille fountain
with a small waterfall.

cut by many windows forming double, triple and quadruple arches on the *piano nobile*. On one side, the structure incorporates a winter garden closed off by another building also placed at a right angle. The interior has been decorated with the greatest simplicity. Some antique pieces of furniture, wall coverings, tapestries, cabinets, sculptures, hanging lights and paintings have been added sparingly to avoid clutter. Here, the owners have opted for comfortable surroundings, creating a perfect place for respite from the hectic life in Florence.

Mythological statues like this
drunken Bacchus stand
in the woods near the pond;
many such spirits inhabit the villas
of Tuscany.

Entirely turned towards the exterior, the rear of the house opens out onto a large terrace overlooking the town of Doccia and offers a splendid view of Sesto and the surrounding hills. The gravel-covered terrace is adorned with palm trees, several parterres of rose bushes and a small central pool. The front façade overlooks a broad English-style lawn that has replaced the original garden since the 19th century. To the right, antique columns surrounded by trees enclose a low basin, giving a slightly romantic touch to the spot. Higher up on the sloping terrain, a central path leads along horizontal parterres ringed with hedges and terra cotta pots of lemon trees.

Two orangeries are located at the end of this path before arriving at the far gates of property. On the other side, an alley neatly carved through immense woods is bordered with cypress trees and ascends towards the distant hillside. The grove of pruned ilexes is greatly appreciated in the summer for the shade it offers. In winter, on special evenings, a very unusual hunting practice took place in former days: the hunters carried bright lanterns into the woods to dazzle thrushes and other small birds and then shot at them with crossbows loaded with bread pellets. Farther up, enclosed by walls since the 19th century, vineyards and olive orchards scatter over the slopes of Mount Acuto, and majestic cypress trees grow as far as the 1500-foot summit.

In the 17th century, the villa was in effect the center of an important agricultural and industrial estate. In addition to the vineyards and olive groves, the Ginori-Lisci owned the fields on the plains below in the valleys of the Zambra and Rimaggio. In 1735, Carlo Andrea founded the third largest porcelain factory in Europe at Doccia. The kaoline necessary for its fabrication came down the Brenta River by barge from Asiago, in Venice, and was then transported by boat to Leghorn before going up the Arno River on a small craft to Porto di Signa, where it was finally pulled by ox-drawn carts to Doccia. Carlo Andrea summoned several decorators from Vienna, such as Ulderico Prucher, who was also an expert in botany and had a large greenhouse for exotic plants built below the garden. In the 19th century, ten huge Italian kilns were installed, each with four levels, to fire and glaze the pottery in addition to finer porcelain.

Villa Ginori-Lisci, although built in the 17th century, has been able to preserve its simplicity in the tradition of the great Humanist ideals of the Renaissance.

The rooms, surmounted by white vaulted ceilings outlined
in gold and stucco motifs and with floors paved
in a geometrical-pattern mosaic avoid the overstatements
so common in the 17th century.

Above:
The plain and austere rear facade of the Villa Rospigliosi
(where the main entrance used to be) was planned
by Bernini in the Roman Baroque style blended
with Tuscan rigor.

Right:
Print by Guiseppe Zocchi, 1774, Florence, Uffizi, Gabinetto
Disegni e Stampe. Originally, the roof was bordered
by a balustrade bearing sixteen Baroque statues (these were
removed in the 19th century).

Veduta della Villa di Lamporecchio di S. E. il S. Duca Rospigliosi.   26.

ROSPIGLIOSI

To the west of Florence in the town of Lamporecchio, Villa Rospigliosi, also known by its old name *Lo Spicchio,* sits on the side of one of the foothills of the Albano Mountain range.

The Rospigliosi, an old family of merchants and bankers, moved to Pistoia in the 13th century. Two centuries later, Milanese Rospigliosi had his *case da signore* built in Lamporecchio among the farms which had once belonged to an ancient monastery. In the 17th century, Giulio Rospigliosi, an exceptionally gifted prelate, having been appointed Bishop of Tarsus, legate and cardinal, finally ascended the papal throne under the name of Clement IX in 1667. His papacy, however, was to last only for two years. This new pope, very attached to his birthplace, decided to transform the *casa* of Lamporecchio into a true palace. Clement IX, sensing that the end of his life was near, confided the hasty transformation of the building to Gianlorenzo Bernini, to whom he had commissioned the statues carrying the Instruments of the Passion on the Ponte Sant'Angelo in Rome. The work on the villa, however, was not completed until after the pope's death, probably around 1675. Bernini, having drawn up the plans, left Mattia de' Rossi, whom he considered his most gifted student, to proceed with the construction.

A slowly ascending avenue bordered by ilexes forming a shady bower leads to the villa's main entrance, formerly in the rear, facing the village of Lamporecchio close to the marshes. In the days of the

The arched entrance way is framed by a molding topped by a Bernini-type scrolled pediment surmounted by Pope Clement IX's coat of arms; in the foreground, two stone watchdogs are seated on the balustrade.

villa's splendor, the visitor made his way through copses of rare trees and scattered fountains, ponds, gazebos and belvederes that have since been replaced by rustic olive groves. Bernini, following Sangallo's and Buontaleni's principles, drew a simple, efficient and rigorous plan with a rectangular central block and two lateral projecting wings of lower height. These wings provided space for terraces protected by balustrades, and low flights of stone steps, both in the front and the rear of the building.

Visitors entering through the majestic main door of the patinated front façade are awed by the boldness and magnificence of the vast oval reception hall. Its decorative composition expands the volume of the room and gives it a rhythm. It is difficult to distinguish the genuine architectural features from those that are merely in trompe-l'œil; multiple twin columns supporting an ornate entablature alternate with niches displaying their own illusionist architectural elements to achieve a spectacular effect of shifting reality. At each side of the room, over the triple doors, scroll pediments flanked by two winged victories are crowned with the coat of arms of Clement IX.

The dramatic oval of the grandiose *salone delle feste* is repeated on the mezzanine and living-quarter levels but without decoration. Each of these halls opens onto three rooms constituting the core of the building. Some of the beautiful coffered ceiling have survived, but most of the rooms have been redone. Two identical spiral staircases connect floors on the northwest and southwest sides of the main block.

The broad expanse of lawn in front of the villa is bordered with hedges and potted lemon trees, and on the right-hand side with outbuildings. At its center, an ornamental pond is highlighted by a fountain in the form of a grinning satyr crouching on a small island of stones and holding a goatskin out of which water spurts.

Over the lawn, past the pond in front of the villa, visitors can admire the family oratory surrounded by trees. This chapel was built on a square plan and, like the villa, its façade displays elements enlivened by horizontal and vertical lines in gray stonework called *pietra serena,* juxtaposed with areas of pale plaster. A few steps lead to a porch crowned by a pediment. Above a semicircular arch reign the coat of arms of the Rospigliosi family. The chapel's beautiful oval interior is entirely decorated with frescos. Double columns and balconies abounding with cherubs adorn the Baroque drum that supports the cupola on which a fresco of the *Ascent of the Virgin Mary into Heaven* has been painted.

Sir Harold Acton expressed his dismay at the dilapidated condition of this superb estate in his book on Tuscan Villas. His fears have since been allayed by the Associazone Provinciale dei Albergatori di Montecatini Terme (the nearby spa town) which has restored it and turned it into a center for banquets and receptions.

The great Baroque hall on the ground floor was probably
decorated by Lodovico Giminiani, who worked at
the Rospigliosi palace in Pistoia. The triangular apertures
in the dome form a star pattern converging towards
the center of the ceiling.

In the main hall, the allegories
on the elliptical dome's
pendentives represent the signs
of the Zodiac and surround
a central fresco of Apollo's chariot
drawn by four horses.

Right:
The chapel, in tones of gray, blue
and yellow, bathed in a soft light
falling sideways on the altar, offers
a vision of serenity and harmony.

Opposite:
The successions of openings,
windows, doors, frames, the
superimposition of planes and the
trompe-l'œil architectural decor
give the illusion of depth—a
process often used in Italy since
the Renaissance.

In the background behind the
satyr, the chapel with its cupola,
probably designed by Bernini at
a later date (c. 1678).

Opposite
The severe façade viewed from
the pond, with its horizontal and
vertical lines created by the simple
rhythmical arrangement
of cornices, quoins and molded
window frames from the basement
to the upper story.

Above and right:
Celle's sober north façade surmounted by the graceful
pediment facing south; to the east a small chapel can
be seen through the trees. Today, the entrance to the house
is on this side.

CELLE

On a hillside to the west of Pistoia in the town of Celle stands a villa bearing the same name. Today, a long path winds through the woods from the main gate past the old farm up to the rear of the house. The original road, however, used to ascend all the way from the valley offering a splendid view of the building's front façade and gardens. It culminated in a circular field flanked by watchtowers on either side where monumental portals gave access to two Italian-style gardens.

These gardens of identical size are enclosed by a low wall graced with scrolls and terra cotta urns. There is a vegetable garden on the left with a niche housing the statue of the beautiful Pomona, goddess of fruits. To the right an alley bordered with azalea bushes enters into yet another garden planted with lemon and orange trees. In the center of the field, a monumental staircase with two curved banisters ascends to the upper level on which the edifice sits. From this vast terrace, the perspective of the original access road to the villa and, in the background, the Rigo River valley, spread out as far as the eye can see. Directly in front of the main façade, a two-tiered stone fountain in the center of a round basin graces the esplanade. On the under side of the first tier, roaring lion heads seem as if they were about to spring. Four massive scrolled pedestals adorn the basin's rim; each supports two stone dolphins, back to back with their bodies inter-twined and their eyes filled with a horribly grimacing expression.

On the lovely ocher-colored main façade, banded rustication underlines the different sections of the building, each three stories

The balustrade of the double staircase that leads up to the piano nobile adorned with splendid stone eagles bearing the Matteini coat of arms since the 19th century.

Below:
Great care has been given to even the smallest detail such as the winged mascarons and pateras that underline windows cut into the basement on the front façade.

Right:
Centered on the front façade above the pediment, the coat of arms of the Matteini displays a plumed helm and a floating ribbon with the inscription: TEMPUS OMNIA VINCIT (Time Conquers All). In the foreground the basins of the 17th-century tiered fountain.

high above a basement. The old 15th-century fortified house was entirely refurbished in the 17th century by the Fabroni, a family of modest ancestry who gained fame from their courage during the war against the Turks. The Fabroni coat of arms hangs on the rusticated quoin to the left of the entrance door. The central block of the building is heightened by an elegantly-designed scrolled pediment surmounted with decorative urns and a bell.

The ensemble gives an impression of refinement thanks to numerous stylized details: little squares in relief around the windows of the second floor, swags on the lintels, shells above the doorway, ornamental bands projecting from the façade imitating window frames...

On the ground floor, an arcade built under the staircase gives direct access to the Fabroniana library, named after Cardinal Carlo Agostino Fabroni, who founded it in 1706. The discrete white stucco that adorns the vaulted ceiling and the lovely pale-green credenza lighten up the room and make it an agreeable place to work.

Along the wall to the right of the building stands a little chapel built in 1703 on a Greek cross plan. The central arch of the serlian portico projecting from the chapel's façade is crowned with the Fabroni coat of arms. The small three-tiered cupola, which is oddly roofed with flat fan-shaped tiles, rises above the triangular pediment. The farm buildings are clustered together on the other side of the esplanade facing the chapel. From this vantage point it is possible to see the rear façade of the house which rises only three stories because of the uneven ground level and, while organized differently from the front façade, is decorated with the same motifs. An addition with a semi-blind portico and two higher lateral blocks projects from this face.

To the east and west of the house behind the chapel and the farm buildings stretches a vast wooded park. At the end of the 19th century, having made a fortune in the United States and having married an American heiress, Giuseppe Matteini bought the property and decided to create an English-style park. Its entranceway, framed by four columns surmounted by vases of flowers, is found to the east of the esplanade. Somewhere in the maze of broad alleys winding under great oaks is the vestige of a little zoo, a Neo-Gothic tea-house and a brick aviary, strangely topped by a pointed cone. A charming wooden bridge over a small artificial lake leads to a treasure island.

Celle is one of the rare 17th-century villas that has been able to preserves its architectural integrity. The presence of two enclosed gardens, the lovely chapel and the great landscaped park combine to render the villa an intimate and delightful place, perfect for an afternoon stroll.

Contemporary sculptures among the trees.

Above:
View of the four columns at the entrance
of the park and the greenhouse overlooking
the enclosed lemon and orange grove.

Center:
The unusual aviary designed by Bartolomeo Sestini
in the 19th century.

A small mock bridge along
romantic woods.

The abandoned zoo surrounded
by contemporary sculpture.

Above:
The small 18th-century chapel.

Center:
A small round temple housing Venus and her
dolphin adorns an islet in the middle of the lake.

An entablature with carved floral patterns and trefoil windows
added in the 20th century give an eccentric touch
to the façade overlooking the park.

IL RIPOSO DEI VESCOVI

Directly north of Florence among a group of houses in the town of San Domenico di Fiesole, sits a villa known today as Villa Nieuwenkamp, but originally called Il Riposo dei Vescovi. This strange name comes from a legend relating how the bishops of Fiesole, who were forced to live in Florence at the time, would stop to rest in this ancient 14th-century *casa colonica* before continuing their exhausting climb to the city.

The first impression of the property is confusing, for the arched stone portal adorned with small carved columns and the face of a Gothic-like monster cannot be identified as belonging to any particular period. This feeling persists throughout the visit and is reinforced by the narration of a curious and eventful history.

In the 16th century, Il Riposo was part of the Villa Rondinelli-Vitelli situated higher up on the hillside. The entire estate was sold in the 19th century to a member of the Borghese family who began to refurbish it. The new owner preserved the tower and the old section of the house that ran along the road and added a perpendicular building that became the main block. Two loggias were constructed, one with semi-circular arches borne on pilasters at the ground-floor level, the other screened by slender columns on the next story. The house was built on different levels following the slope of the hillside. Several extravagant transformations were made at the end of the 19th century by the Swiss architect, Zurcher, who had the incredible idea of instal-

The front façade remodeled in the 19th century in a typical
Renaissance style.

Buddha, the true *genius loci* of
Nieuwenkamp's paradise.

Not satisfied with all the objects
he brought back from the Orient,
Nieuwenkamp created his own.
His delusions of grandeur made
him affix dates on every object.

ling a chalet-like appendage to the top of the tower. The property was bought in 1926 by the Francioni family which still lives there today.

That same year, the Dutch painter and engraver, W.O.J. Nieuwenkamp—disciple of Gauguin and a rather unusual person—lived there in between his trips to Indonesia and throughout Europe. He decided to express his love for Italy by transforming the villa into a personal museum. Until his death in 1950, he continued to imprint the villa with oriental touches. He had boatloads of bas-reliefs as well as various and sundry objects transported from Indonesia and then scattered them around the house.

A bronze gong used by a servant to announce meals hangs next to the entrance. The front hall is decorated with ceramic bas-reliefs from Bali and oriental-style marble mirrors with beautiful arabesques, all assembled by Nieuwenkamp and marked with his initials. The Francioni family, who cherish his memory, exhibit his sketch pad that shows details of each corner of the house, each new transformation, as well as many landscapes and picturesque scenes of Indonesia and Italy.

Most of the doors are crowned by semi-circular stone arches sculpted with geometric patterns. All the rugs, chests, dishes and miniature objects have an oriental flavor. Curiously, the walls around the chimneys are surrounded with Indonesian and Italian bas-reliefs, sculptures and various medallions, (dolphins, angels' heads, Madonnas) picked up in Florentine antique stores.

The hall leads into a large room with tall arched windows looking out over a big pool of greenish water with an antique sarcophagus at the far end. Beyond, the wall is bordered with cypress trees. The exterior walls, stairs and roofs, a helter-skelter combination of stone, brick, tile and marble, give a slipshod impression. On the left, preceding the salon, a small gothic-style loggia with pointed arches, small columns and Ionic capitals open onto the garden.

To the right of the pool, a path skirting the bamboo parterre offers a panoramic view and leads to the park on the lower level. There, a staircase gives access to a large terrace surrounded by a balustrade and adorned with a small fountain.

From this spot the park spreads out as far as the eye can see. Created in part in the 19th century, it was enlarged by Nieuwenkamp between 1926 and 1935. This immense garden, split into two parts by an alley of cypresses that descends in a straight line to the surrounding walls is crisscrossed by scores of horizontal paths. Each intersection displays a different ornament; at the first level, two feminine busts; at the second, an oriental-style fountain; at the third, a wisteria-covered pergola overlooking a lawn-tennis court and large terra cotta Etruscan urns (a souvenir from the digs undertaken by Nieuwenkamp in Fiesole) surmount the embankment of a terrace. Along the main alley, past the fruit orchard and vegetable garden, before reaching the fourth level, stands an elliptical clearing fringed by cypresses and graced by

The arched windows of the grand salon, between unusual
terra cotta bamboo-shaped downspouts, overlook the pool
behind the house; the ground floor is surmounted by a terrace
with a balustrade.

The wisteria-covered pergola where architectural elements and
natural surroundings follow the principles of the 16th-century
Tuscan garden.

The fountain embedded in the enclosing wall ends the visit.

Below:
The lovely perspective of the central alley running down the
entire length of the garden; an oriental inspired fountain with
a carved shaft at the charming crossing.

One of the garden's most beautiful spots combining,
in an eclectic fashion, Etruscan tombstones and vases
in terra cotta with a wisteria-covered pergola and a terraced
wall decorated with different artifacts created by
Nieuwenkamp.

Left:
A curious spiraled column dominates the center of the alley
and marks the fourth level.

three fluted columns. The fifth level features a fountain embedded in the enclosing garden wall.

There is a choice of itineraries back up to the house, either along the central avenue or up lateral paths. The left-hand path winds under a vine-covered pergola, and then follows a shaded passageway and runs past Nieuwenkamp's tombstone. The artist had it laid before his death. Although he is not buried here, his soul doubtless remains in this garden, guarded by the statue of a thoughtful Buddha.

The façade seen from the road through olive groves and majestic fir trees. To the left, the path bordered with hedges running along the outbuildings up to the villa. To the right, the terrace overlooking the entire Arno River valley.

Right:
Engraving by Giuseppe Zocchi, 1744, Uffici, Gabinetto Nazionale della Stampe, Florence; the villa has hardly changed since the 18th century.

Villa di Gamberaia del Sig.ʳ Marchese Scipione Capponi.

GAMBERAIA

Villa Gamberaia lies on a slope of the Settignano hills to the northeast of Florence. Past the semi-circular gates, an avenue of cypress trees leads to the elevated terrace on which the house stands.

The 14th-century *casa colonica* was built in the center of a large agricultural estate by an order of Benedictine nuns from San Martino a Mensola. In 1610, it was taken over by Zanobi di Andrea Lapi, who decided to transform the convent into a sumptuous edifice and to add service buildings. The two-storied structure built around a central courtyard was lengthened on two sides by double-arched walls. One of these arcades links the main block to a small chapel embedded in an outbuilding and the other to the adjoining garden.

The villa's entrance is on the west side. The cream-colored façade enhanced by a large rusticated door, simple trabeated windows and banded quoins in *pietra serena,* retains a definite Tuscan flavor. In front, the vast grassy terrace is marked off by a parapet crowned with urns and moss-covered stone dogs and lions typical of traditional Florentine gardens. This vantage point commands a vast prospect of rolling hills dotted with olive groves and cypresses and, in the background, the valley of the Arno River bathed in soft blue light.

A loggia set in the south wall of the villa looks out over the remarkable water parterre. Laid out by the landscape architects Martino Porcinai and Luigi Messeri between 1905 and 1913 for Princess Giovanna Ghyka, this garden enchants the eye with its

The marvelous garden off the southern façade. Pink azaleas
and geraniums flower amid boxwood topiary, adding colorful
touches to the dominating lush greens.

Center right:
"There, all is beauty, luxury, calm and voluptuousness."
Baudelaire.

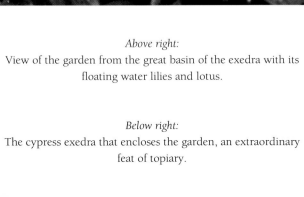

Above right:
View of the garden from the great basin of the exedra with its
floating water lilies and lotus.

Below right:
The cypress exedra that encloses the garden, an extraordinary
feat of topiary.

115

On either side of the central path,
charming stone cherubs peep out
from boxwood topiary.

Right:
From the loggia, one of the most
idyllic hanging gardens of
Tuscany; as far as the eye can see,
olive groves and shimmering
golden fields extend into the gray-
blue haze of the hills as rendered
by Raphael, Bellini and
Pinturicchio.

rigorous geometric patterns and multiple perspectives which make it seem bigger than it really is.

Paths paved in a mosaic of pebbles divide the splendid garden sheltered behind high hedges of clipped boxwood. Four elongated symmetrical water parterres frame a small round central basin sporting a mushroom-shaped fountain in rustic stonework. The shimmering sheets of water are rimmed in gray stone and fringed by ewe-hedge topiary. At the far end, stone animals and terra cotta urns stretch along a low wall.

Behind a boxwood maze, a theatrical exedra of high cypresses pierced by arches closes the garden. One of these arches leads onto a small terrace. A stately pine tree provides a shady resting place and a bench allows the enraptured visitor to sit and admire once again the marvelous landscape.

A lush bowling green travels from one end of the garden to the other, past the villa which is bordered on one side by a high wall once

The stairs leading from the grotto
to the lemon-tree garden

Right:
The stunning perspective of the
grassy walk bordering the
outbuildings and the villa; the
buildings are joined by two high
arches.

Opposite:
The glorious mauve of the
hydrangea bushes matches the pale
pink pebbles of the rustic stone
grotto; terra cotta statues of Tuscan
peasants in traditional costume are
displayed in niches.

decorated by frescos. Across from the villa's east entrance, a small path leads into a secret garden where large pots of pink and mauve flowers enliven the subtle colors of a grotto's mosaic and rustic stonework. This charming spot is surrounded by a balustrade and displays stone busts on pedestals, obelisks and terra cotta urns. Stairs run up and down on both sides; the one on the left leads to a lemon garden on an upper level with an orangery for the winter. These are the only areas that have remained unchanged since the 17th century.

On the right, a shady paths winds through an ilex grove and leads back to the bowling green at the far end of the outbuildings. Then, a promenade under cypress trees provides access to a broad esplanade closed off by a large *rocaille* wall, embellished with more mosaic and rustic stonework holding the Fountain of Neptune. Benches embedded on either side of the embankment flank an arch-shaped artificial grotto decorated with stalactites. Water drips from mossy rocks, and, inside a niche, a stucco relief depicts Neptune brandishing his trident.

Villa Gamberaia is a rare jewel. Its smooth and harmonious façade blends perfectly with the beautiful ensemble of gardens, the most perfect of which is without doubt the south water parterre. Although more recent, the villa is the most evocative of the spirit of Tuscany and of the Renaissance. It is also a model of preservation. It offers an unforgettable panorama of the farmed countryside and the surrounding hills.

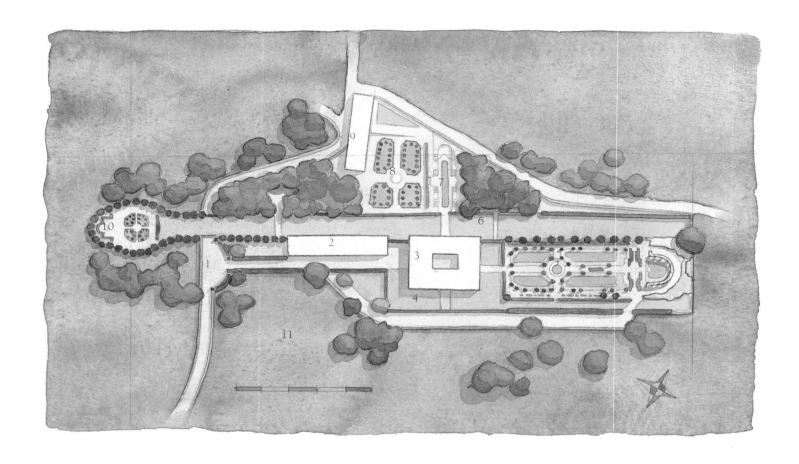

Plan of the villa de Gamberaia
today from G. Mader and L.
Neubert-Mader, Jardins Italiens,
Fribourg, 1987:

1) entrance, 2) outbuildings, 3) villa, 4) terrace,

5) garden, 6) grassy walk, 7) rhododendron garden,

8) lemon tree garden, 9) lemon house, 10) Fountain

of Neptune, 11) olive groves

Opposite:
The garden's finale, a shady
clearing ideal for a moment
of rest, also the site of Neptune's
grotto.

The elegant north façade enhanced by Baroque motifs
and the wall enclosing the garden, running eastward.

LA PIETRA

The entrance to Villa La Pietra is found at n° 120, Via Bolognese on the road out of Florence. An long alley of cypress trees runs through olive groves before reaching the entrance esplanade, where, above trimmed circular hedges, the elegant silhouette of the house emerges.

The 14th-century villa passed into the hands of the Sassetti family, bankers and philanthropists at the Medici's service, in the 15th century. They sold it a century later to the Capponi. In the beginning of the 17th century, Cardinal Luigi Capponi, after serving as pontifical legate, decided to retire to La Pietra and gave his property a Baroque appearance, more in keeping with the times. The building has preserved its proportions and original square plan around a central courtyard, but its exterior aspect was entirely modified by two architects, Carlo Fontana and Giuseppe Ruggieri, who had already designed the Capponi family palace in Florence. They added projecting Baroque elements in *pietra serena*, with pediments and moldings above the windows, wrought-iron balconies on the *piano nobile,* and a balustrade adorned with urns on the roof, without removing the earlier motifs.

The original *cortile*, decorated by a Mannerist fountain crowned with a satyr, has been covered and transformed into a large two-story high *salone* with an elliptical suspended staircase. Many of the rooms have not changed since the 15th century and still bear the Sassetti coat of arms on their vaulted ceilings.

Preceding page and above:
View of the garden in front of the south façade blending
Renaissance and Baroque motifs; the central doorway with its
16th-century lintel, later surmounted by a Baroque segmental
pediment underneath a wrought-iron balcony; near the roof,
the Capponi coat of arms.

Opposite, above:
The low wall bordering the first level of the terrace displays
Baroque statues overlooking the west parterre.

Opposite, below:
Some of the curious mythological figures that inhabit
the garden.

Inside the grotto hidden in the
woods, now a summer pavilion;
a luxurious rocaille decor
of pebbles and seashells.

Below:
Two monumental statues
temporarily housed in an
outbuilding at the Villa.

Sir Harold Acton's magnificent library.

Below:
Each corner of the house contains a prestigious collection of antiques.

The sumptuous pergola where ivory-colored Banks roses
perfume the air.

When Arthur Acton, the father of the present owner, bought the villa at the beginning of the century, the whole garden had been done over in the English-landscape style. He decided that it was more suitable for a Tuscan garden to return to a more formal Italian style and imagined what it would have looked like in the 17th century. He redesigned the layout, planning it around an imaginary axis that extended down the hillside's three levels ending at the entrance portal. Afterwards, he did his best to assemble a collection of statues, sculptures and architectonic decoration from the 17th and 18th centuries which he placed around the garden according to his fancy.

An unusual garden lies to the right of the house, beside a wisteria-covered wall on which curious antique sculptures have been arranged. Monumental stone statues representing mythological gods and goddesses are scattered randomly around a parterre of classic trimmed boxwood. The terrace fringed with more statues and flower pots turns around the house, forming the upper level of the garden. On the balustrade Athena, Bacchus, Hercules and Apollo, draped in flowing robes, strike various poses giving the impression of actors on a stage.

Two staircases behind the house lead to the level below; here, the whole garden is also enclosed by a low wall lined with further statuary and planted with tall cypress trees. In the center of a cone-trimmed hedge, rises a lovely fountain overflowing with water lilies. Farther away, past the wide stairs paved with mosaics, and beyond a columned pergola covered with Banks roses, lies a small esplanade. Two double columns surmounted by broken arches and flanked by two statues mark the entrance to a green theater. From this spot spreads forth the scenic exedra with its parterre of boxwood planted in concentric circles against a background of Corinthian columns forming yet another pergola around a central fountain.

On either side of the main axis of the garden, perpendicular paths lead to small enclosed lawns or to round clearings enclosed by hedges in which statues stand alone or in groups in an architectural setting: an arch in *pietra serena*, or a niche imbedded in a natural boxwood backdrop. These intimate cloistered spaces inspire the imagination and invite daydreaming, possibly even playing. The statues of Venetian courtesans and gentlemen sculpted by Francesco Bonazza seem to belong to a theater scene by Goldoni; Venus rising from the sea was surely inspired by Botticelli's painting; Hercules' sad countenance was sculpted by Orazio Marinali; Apollo's pursuit of Daphne, who finally turns into a bay tree, and Psyche tenderly embracing Eros in the small round Temple of Love, give the garden a frivolous charm and festive gaiety.

Sunny clearings alternate with wooded areas, but the dominant colors are the green of the trees, topiary and lawn and the gray of the statues, columns and arches. There are almost no flowers, no touches of color to disrupt a harmony that emphasizes the fantastic character

One of the many scenic terraces.

of the perspectives and the strange *mise en scène*. Many of the stage-like terraces express a certain melancholy, perhaps due to the Actons' attachment to English ways and things, well-suited to poetic musing.

It is easy to get lost, for the garden is immense and offers many surprises. On the left side of the façade, across the wall adorned with *rocaille* motifs, lies an old 17th-century secret garden transformed today into a vegetable patch. A cheerful fountain crowned by a cherub riding a dolphin rises out of a circle of hedges trimmed into arcades.

La Pietra remains a rare example of the successful re-creation of 17th-century theatrical garden in all its splendor. The present owner has perfectly blended "natural Nature" with "artificial Nature" in a very personal and original manner.

The magnificent exedra; each
element—whether sculptural,
architectural or natural—has been
carefully put in place.

I Tatti

Villa I Tatti stands to the northeast of Florence near Villa Gamberaia. After crossing the Mensola river, the old wrought-iron doorway—formerly the main entrance to the estate—sits at the bottom of an straight alley bordered by cypress trees forming a breathtaking perspective that converges on the right side of the house. Today, it is necessary to walk around the property to the left and enter the central courtyard surrounded by ancient outbuildings.

Through an opening in a wisteria-covered wall, a little secret garden decorated with parterres of boxwood and heather abuts an elegant row of scrolled arches. The central arch is imbedded with a niche holding a round urn surmounted by a grimacing mask. A straight staircase leads from here down to a small esplanade enlivened by superb earthen-ware pots of bright azaleas in front of the warm ocher-colored west façade of the house. To the right an altogether unexpected avenue bordered by ilex trees descends a gradual slope into small woods. This walk is very unlike the traditional rectilinear Italian alley preceding the entrance of a villa. Of a more English concept, it respects the topography of the terrain, yet seems to lead nowhere. It runs down, however, to a small hidden basin adorned by statues and spanned by a narrow arch of metal trellises, shielded from the sun.

Farther on, a little door through a wisteria-covered wall on the southwest corner of the property opens onto a lovely garden

The enclosed garden in front of the south façade, passage underneath the orangery leads to the modern garden.

Left:
The east façade of I Tatti that used to be the main entrance.

133

The south façade from the 15th-century garden, a paradisiac
enclosure that evokes the old Roman hortus conclusus,
extolled by the Humanists of the Renaissance.

Right:
The garden is organized into parterres of green boxwood
surrounding large olive trees and beds of multicolored flowers.

surrounded with high walls and closed off by the long façade of the orangery. From here, parterres descend in successive terraces, forming the only section of the garden that dates from the 16th century when the estate belonged to the Zatti family. The central alley, edged with potted lemon trees and statues in passive stances, leads down to the brightly colored roof of the orangery surmounted by pots of pink geraniums.

From the ivy-covered central arch crowned with stone jars unfolds an astonishing vista. Man-sized hedges of cypress border a long garden with parterres of boxwood carefully trimmed into various geometric shapes. Double curved stairs enveloping a small basin descend to an alley entirely paved with a superb finely-edged mosaic of pebbles. Step by step the path leads down through the hedges until reaching a vast lawn encasing two water-lily basins. Still lower, another double staircase leads to an ilex grove. A long row of benches affords a moment of rest to contemplate the warm colors of the house and contrasts with the different greens of the tall cypress, the ivy and the topiary of the parterres.

This extraordinary ensemble was created entirely between 1908 and 1915 by two landscape artists, Cecil Pinsent and Geoffrey Scott, who developed a contemporary conception of architectural gardening inspired by the Italian Renaissance. These two men were summoned by the owner of the villa, the great art historian and art collector, Bernard Berenson (1865-1959). Berenson had been living in Italy since 1887 when he discovered Villa I Tatti and decided to restore it in 1905. At the beginning of the century, the house was entirely reconstructed around a central courtyard to conform to its original square plan and to return to its 16th-century appearance. Only the

The alley that skirts the east façade; the typical potted lemon
trees of the Tuscan garden was one of the Trees of the Golden
Apples of the mythical Hesperides Garden; the lemon trees
has always symbolized eternal springtime.

section of the garden behind the orangery was laid out; the rest of the grounds were left untouched. Berenson found inspiration in a book by Edith Wharton (*Italian Villas and Their Gardens*. New York: 1903) which had captivated all the English and Americans enamored with Italian landscape.

These are the words that he used to described his well-loved garden: "I have a garden too, as I mentioned earlier. Unless it pours with rain I run through it at least once a day, to taste the air, to listen to the sound of birds and streams, to admire the flowers and trees. (…) Each day as I look, I wonder where my eyes were yesterday. Why did I not perceive the beauty of the lichen-trimmed tree-trunk as gorgeous as an Aztec or Maya mosaic; of that moss of a soft emerald that beds your eye as reposefully as the greens in a Giorgione or Bonifazio…." (*Sketch for a Self-Portrait*. New York: Pantheon Books, 1949.)

Berenson, a specialist of the Italian Renaissance, has contributed greatly to spread the splendors of Quattrocento art, especially in the United States, with his many seminal works; e.g. *Italian Painters of the Renaissance*. 4 vols. 1894-1907; *Drawings of the Florentine Painters*. 3 vols. 1938. He put together a prodigious collection of 14th and 15th-century paintings (Giotto, Bernardo Daddi, Simone Martini, Giovanni Bellini, etc…) as well as an imposing library. In 1959, Berenson gave the villa and its contents to Harvard University, where he had been a student. The villa, transformed into a center for Italian Renaissance studies, now takes in researchers and students from all over the world.

I Tatti remains a charming place infused with the love Berenson lavished upon it and the devotion his disciples still bestow on it. It is a place of scholarship and a hymn to the beauty and ideals of the Italian Renaissance.

The amazing scenic prospect of the
long alley flanked by cypress trees
that leads to the old entrance of
the east façade.

Left:
The ivy-clad orangery marks off
the limit between the 15th-century
garden—visible through the
arcade—and the modern parterre.
To symbolize Nature's abundance,
stone fruit baskets have been
placed here and there
on the curvilinear perron
above the staircase.

The remarkable south parterre; in the background two solitary
cypress trees emerging from the misty hills in front of the
town of San Martino a Mensola seem to prolong the prospect.

Opposite above:
The south façade flanked by cypress trees dominates the
perfect symmetry of grandiose parterre.

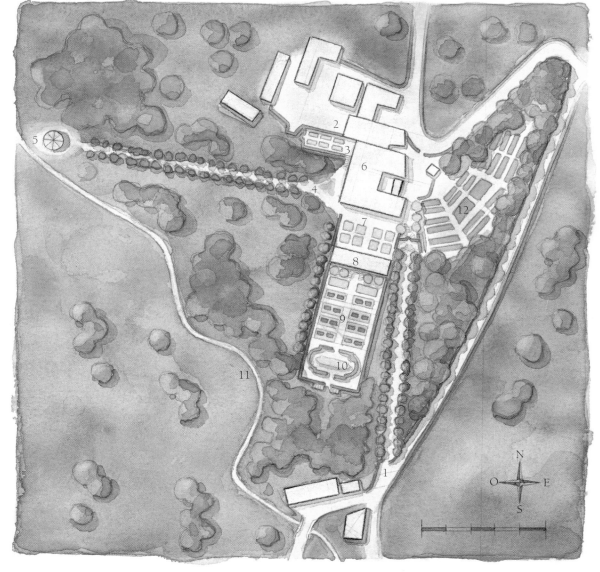

The plan of I Tatti today after G.
Mader and L. Neubert-Mader,
Jardins Italiens, Fribourg, 1987:

1) the old entrance, 2) the actual entrance,

3) Garden with the Mask, 4) Alley of the ilex grove,

5) basin, 6) house, 7) 15th-century garden,

8) orangery, 9) modern parterre, 10) basin,

11) Mensola river, 12) vegetable garden

The extraordinary vaulted parking space beneath Pietro Porcinai's suspended garden; an attractive pavement of black and white pebbles underlines the skylight wells and the alley leading to the staircase.

Right:
The west façade of Il Roseto in the setting sun.

IL ROSETO

Villa Il Roseto (The Rose Garden) is hidden away in the town of Arcetri just south of Florence. The driveway leads through the gates directly into an underground garage. In 1965, the Benelli family summoned the landscape architect Pietro Porcinai (1910-1986) to create parking spaces without destroying any section of the garden.

Porcinai, the son of Villa Gamberaia's gardener, initiated at a very early age to formal Italian gardens, put his art to practice in Italy as well as in the United States, Spain and Saudi Arabia. Drawing inspiration from 16th and 17th-century grottos, he had the clever idea of elevating the front section of the garden to accommodate a covered parking lot. This irregularly-shaped area lies under cupolas decorated with inconspicuous graffito motifs and supported by simple concrete columns. An attractive pavement with patterns in black-and-white-pebbled mosaic repeats the circular shapes overhead. The expanse is bright and well-lit from openings along the sides and through skylights at the summit of the concrete cupolas. A large tree planted in a plot of earth grows surrealistically through the garage roof with only the trunk visible. Tendrils of ivy hang like sheet of running water down the sides of a cylinder-shaped well that encloses a staircase. An impression of coolness is accentuated further by the murmuring of a little fountain. The spiral staircase ascends into a horse-shoe-shaped hedge of clipped boxwood leading to the hanging garden in front of the house.

One of the many flowery garden
walks that wind up the hillside.

Left:
The west façade seen from
Porcinai's parterre with the circular
hedge hiding the staircase down
to the garage.

The sloping garden with the hills
in the background.

Above:
The splendid view of the distant
hills with the Torre del Gallo on
the right of the fishpond.

This terrace was laid out in a contemporary style by Porcinai, but inspired by the Renaissance with Italian-style parterres of boxwood and stretches of mowed lawn. A concrete path encircles a plot of grass that is centered around a skylight protected by a wrought-iron banister; it repeats the circular design of the underground cupolas. Several beds, overflowing with flowers, add touches of color to the harmony of the greens and grays. Huge oak trees provide the sunny terrace with shade and a round fishpond with a fluted concrete rim closes off the garden. From the parapet bordering the fishpond, a vast panorama unfolds, commanding a view of the neighboring hillside in the distance, the city of Florence to the north and the large sloping garden to the south.

The salmon-colored façade overlooking the parterre was pierced by a modern Renaissance-style rusticated doorway at the same period. The old 17th-century house, entirely refurbished in the 19th and 20th centuries, has preserved the original north façade elevation with the downstairs windows underlined by cornices of gray stone and supported by consoles.

Inside, the rooms are both spacious and luminous and have kept their Renaissance style with moldings around the main doors in *pietra serena* and small wooden doors and coffered ceilings. Wood dominates the hall too, furnished with a heavy table and a magnificent mahogany bookshelf overflowing with old books. This rustic charm is highlighted by dark rugs and tapestries representing satyrs playing musical instruments. Engraved portraits of young women hang on the walls. The pastel-colored salon proudly displays Bohemian-glass goblets on a pedestal table and paintings on wood from the 14th and 15th centuries. The owners, who are also art lovers, have furnished all the rooms in perfect taste and have turned it into a beautiful and comfortable year-round dwelling.

The terrace off the salon overlooks the large garden whose layout has made the most of a sloping hillside. Little ivy-covered stairs lead down to the original level of the villa, forming yet another terrace planted with rhododendrons, geraniums and hedges of cypress. On the right a small path winds down to the magnificent rose garden that gives the property its name. The walk continues past the parking space entrance, across fields planted with olive trees and along alleys edged by blue, yellow, white and red tufts of lavender, daffodils, wild flowers and climbing roses.

Il Roseto remains the best example of a modern interpretation of a Renaissance villa thanks to a landscape architect who knew how to reconcile the needs of the actual owners with the Florentine Humanist tradition. The suspended parterres, the unforgettable panorama and the vast gardens running down the hillside have turned this villa into a quiet and charming abode, a place to escape from the hectic life of Florence.

The geometric parterre seen from the fishpond; the small plot
of grass with a skylight permitting light to enter the garage.

The ground-floor salon. The elegant coffee table in pietra dura
marquetry displays a collection of Russian saltcellars and silver
cigarette cases.

Right:
The south façade's staircase leading to the various terraces.

The severe façade of Villa Mansi

In the 15th century, the territory belonging to the Republic of Lucca could not be compared with that of Florence. It covered a small circle spreading northward to Castelnuovo—except for the enclave of Pietransanta—and eastward to the border of Pescia. But this region's international banking and commerce—the silk trade in particular—could hold its own against that of Florence and began to decline only in the 17th century. *Nouveaux-riches* merchants built villas in the countryside to proclaim their power, prestige and wealth. As early as the 13th century the Buonvisi family owned more than a dozen properties, including Torrigiani. After centuries of fratricidal struggles for power between the Guelfs (partisans of the Pope) and the Ghibellines (partisans of the German Emperor), Lucca finally achieved domestic harmony under Imperial protection in the 16th century, and the construction of villas expanded.

One of the distinctive features of Luccan villas is that of having discarded all traces of their original medieval structure. Their appearance is definitely Renaissance or Baroque, with no similarity whatsoever to a farm or fortified house like the first Medicean villas. The great designer of Luccan villas, Benedetto Saminiati, was responsible for several of Lucca's palaces. Often it was a member of the city's nobility who decided on the design of the edifice and played the role of architect; this was the case of Abbot Paolo Cenami at Mansi, and of Ottaviano Diodati and Romano Garzoni at Garzoni. The influence of Florentine architecture became apparent in the first half of the 16th century: Giuliano da Sangallo's architectural model for Villa Poggio a Caiano seems to have been welcomed in Lucca. This tendency lasted into the 17th century, a period when Luccan architecture found its own style, nonetheless. Several features irrefutably characterized the Luccan villas: the monumental staircase outside the building that ascends to the elevated main floor above a basement, thus creating space for kitchens and other services; the serlian arcades, Doric or Tuscan columns and rusticated pilasters that articulate the loggias; the gray of Golfolina stone that contrasts with the whitewash and red bricks; the refined Mannerism of the façade's various details that create a picturesque decor. The perspectives painted in fresco were borrowed from Bolognese artists such as Angelo Michele Colonna in Garzoni.

Above:
Villa Torrigiani in front of the English-style lawn. The name
of the architect who designed the theater-like façade in
the 17th century remains unknown.

Right:
The front façade through the majestic portal.

TORRIGIANI

Villa Torrigiani lies to the northeast of Lucca, near Pescia, just outside of the town of Camigliano. At the end of a wide alley bordered by immense cypress trees, the majestic silhouette of the house emerges into view standing out against the outline of the misty hills in the distance. A monumental portal opens onto a vast lawn bordered with trees where a typically 19th-century English-style garden has replaced the French-inspired 17th-century parterres that used to stretch out on both sides of the building. These apparently were designed by Le Nôtre himself, on his way back from a trip to Rome. Only the two irregularly-shaped basins survive from this period.

The building was erected in the second half of the 16th century and originally belonged to the Buonvisi family. At the beginning of the 17th century it passed into the hands of the Santini family which transformed the house by remodeling the façades in a typically Mannerist style. Smoothness and roughness alternate dramatically, demonstrating a clever handling of rustications with the juxtaposition of yellow tufa and gray stone. The façade is pierced by two serlian arched porticos supported by columns at the ground-floor level and by rusticated pilasters on the first floor. These are flanked by statues and surmounted by the empaled coat of arms of the Santini and Torrigiani families. On either side of the first-floor portico, the façade is set a little farther back, making room for a terrace with a balustrade adorned with smaller pieces of sculptures. The same motifs are

The grand entrance hall with its sumptuous decoration on two
of the trompe-l'œil cornices. In perspective on the Baroque
ceiling: pots of flowers and pieces of material, dolphins and
garland, shackled slaves and cherubs.

Detail of the vault in a ground-floor room.

repeated around the other terraces, above the cornice of the third floor and above the attic. The ensemble is topped with a domed aedicule surmounted by a small globe. Arches, niches, medallions, windows, balustrades and statues of various sizes rhythmically punctuate the exuberant façade. In spite of this, the building shows perfect symmetry and gives an impression of serenity and peace. During the same period, two projecting wings were added to the rear of the house.

A large fan-shaped staircase ascends to the grand entrance hall entirely covered with Baroque frescos painted in the 17th century. The central fresco depicts *The Apotheosis of Aurelian* as he is carried up to heavens in great chaos. The paintings on the wall by Vincenzo Dandini (*The Battle of the Amazons Against the Romans* and *The Triumph of Aurelian Over the Queen of Zenobia Shackled With Gold Chains*) bear witness to the same prolific frenzy.

The other rooms on the ground and first floors are grandiose with their abundance of luxury. The same type of architectural displays in trompe-l'œil adorn the vaults of the ceilings, and white stucco motifs on a gold background enhanced by wall coverings literally coat the walls. A beautiful collection of 16th and 17th-century paintings in heavy gold frames (*The Last Supper at Emmaus* by

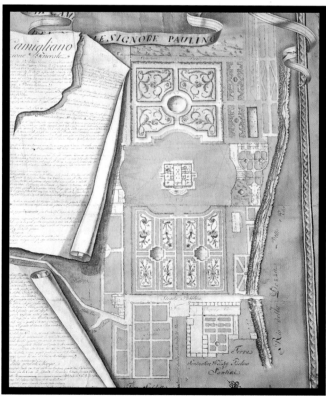

Above left:
The arch through the wall leading to the Grotto of the Seven Winds.

Below left:
Plan of Villa Torrigiani in the 18th century, hanging in one of the downstairs rooms. The house in the center was then bordered on both sides by French-style parterres laid out around two small basins, on the right the garden closed in by the Grotto of the Seven Winds, and the large basin

Above:
The secret garden leading to the Grotto of the Seven Winds
surmounted by the statue of Flora.

Above right:
One of the lovely antique busts decorating the wall of the
secret garden.

Below right:
One of the winged statues of the Seven Winds.

A mascaron underlining one of the niches of the entrance portal.

Pontormo, others by Guercino, Domenichino, Francesco Albani, Salvator Rosa, Bernardo Strozzi and Poussin) was added in 1816 to the already rich array when the villa came into the hands of the Torrigiani family after the marriage of Vittoria Santini to Pietro Guadagni, Marquis Torrigiani. Furniture fills up every available space, crowding rugs, screens, chairs and armchairs, divans, sofas and beds, as well as tables, pianos, harpsichords, desks, cabinets and chests of drawers into every corner; each of these in turn holds precious objects (Chinese porcelain vases, dishes, small chests, religious artifacts). The most impressive rooms are the bedroom furnished with festooned canopy beds from Lucca, the dining room with a collection of Meissen and Capodimonte porcelain and the library filled with old volumes of architectural plans and whose walls are covered with 17th-century French engravings (views of cities, portraits of famous people, scenes of power).

The grounds harbor a totally enchanting Italian-style sunken garden entirely enclosed in sculpture-laden walls, the only remaining vestiges from the 17th century. Although perfectly scaled in miniature, it was laid out in a very grand fashion. It is easy to imagine the beautiful ladies dressed in their seventeenth-century finery descending the graceful double staircase to stroll through the beds of flowers. A feat of engineering, undoubtedly conceived as a practical joke very much in vogue at the time, allowed their host to imprison them in his secret garden by raising a veritable sheet of water from fountains concealed in the highest steps of the staircase and from sprays hidden among the pebble-mosaics along the whole length of the garden. When at last his guests thought they could take shelter in the *rocaille* Grotto of the Seven Winds at the far end, a real deluge awaited them there, forcing them to run up the stairs to the terrace above, only to receive a final drenching from a wreathed statue-*cum*-fountain of the nymph Flora.

The villa and the vestiges of one of the grandest Luccan families have been well preserved thanks to public funds. The lavish secret gardens, originally designed for amusement, and the sumptuous decorations of the house, although modified in the 19th century in an Empire style, give a true picture of the lifestyle of feasts, banquets and receptions that befitted the Luccan villa owner of this period.

The grotto bathed in shadowy light whose
waterworks still enchant the visitor.

At the edge of the woods, a large basin and balustrade adorned with statues.

Opposite and above:
The lovely double staircase with many banisters and landings leading to the large basin, hides grottos in its embankment.

Above and right:
View of Villa Mansi's radiant front façade, Muzio Oddi's
masterpiece in the Mannerist style of Lucca.

MANSI

Villa Mansi stands near Villa Torrigiani in Segromigno. Past the main gate, a path crosses a little bridge over a stream near a small bamboo-covered island into a courtyard surrounded by ancient outbuildings, and from there leads directly to the garden.

On the left, a charming and picturesque statue of a hunter and his hound catches the eye, above a bed of boxwood and flowers. The path follows the winding stream that flows over a ramp of mossy stones before disappearing underground. Then comes a noble alley bordered with high hedges of bay trees and delightful statues placed at regular intervals; these stone female figures generously offer Nature's blessings of wheat and fruit to the passer-by. The alley opens onto a large irregularly-shaped fishpond with spurting water, ringed by a balustrade enlivened with potted red geraniums and eight large statues of antique gods and goddesses. It is said that the ghost of beautiful Lucida Mansi, who sold her soul to the devil to preserve her youth, has been seen there upon occasion during the full moon.

Farther along, a small, almost-hidden ornamental pool and a strange artificial grotto emerge from a wooded grove; the *rocaille* arches provide a remarkable backdrop for the exquisite figure of the goddess Diana surprised in her bath with her companions. These two pools are the only remains of a garden planned between 1725 and 1732 by the Baroque landscape designer and world-famous architect Filippo Juvara,

The raised main floor opens onto a portico
with three serlian arches framing graceful
statues.

One of the façade's sensual allegorical
figures mischievously observes a satyr
playing the pipes of Pan.

appointed to the service of Victor Amedeus II of Savoy—the new King
of Sicily and Sardinia. In front of the building, Juvara designed two
gardens with pergolas, fountains, espalier fruit trees and a clock
pavilion for the owner of the villa, Ottavio Guido Mansi.

At the beginning of the 19th century, the gardens were replaced
by an open field in the English-landscape style. This space, bordered
by a broad canopy of trees, constitutes a pleasant preamble to the villa.
The majestic silhouette of the house, with its gradation of blue-grays
stands out noticeably against the greens of the lawn and of the pine
and fir trees all around, and blends harmoniously with the blue-gray
of the hills in the background.

The ancient 16th-century villa belonged to the Benedetti family
before being bought by the Cenami. In 1634-1635, Countess Felice

Above and middle:
The jewel-like ornamental pool ringed with a delicate balustrade and graced by statues of antique gods and goddesses, is surrounded by age-old oaks.

Bottom:
The strange setting of an artificial grotto dedicated to the goddess Diana.

Cenami and her brother, Abbot Paolo Cenami, commissioned the architect Muzio Oddi da Urbino, who had built the city walls of Lucca, to overhaul the building entirely. Oddi created another façade and added a slightly set-back story to the central block. The rhythmical treatment resulting from these modifications is very satisfying. The serlian motif of the monumental portico on the ground floor is repeated around the central window on the upper story. In the same manner, the eight statues between the Doric columns on both levels harmonize with the medallions under grotesque masques sculpted on the spandrels.

The slightly lower wings are enhanced by the windows of the *piano nobile,* each adorned with engaged balconies and open-segmental pediments, each crowned with a bust. In 1742, the Mansi family, already owners since 1675, added a final touch with an engaged balustrade around the roof, surmounted by yet more statues. All these surfaces were articulated together through the arrangement of the openings, projections and contrasting materials of the various cornices, entablatures, statues and columns to achieve an interesting and animated effect.

A symmetrical double staircase guarded by stone dogs leads to the portico. The sumptuous salon is adorned with gilded decoration, frames, paintings and frescos from the neoclassic period; the ceiling depicts trompe-l'œil mythological figures, medallions and atlantes which appear to support the vault. Between 1784 and 1792, while in Rome, Stefano Tofanelli painted several large canvases illustrating the glory of Apollo. These paintings were then transported to the Villa Mansi and integrated into the decor. They describe the *Judgment of Midas* and the *Death of Marsyas,* and over the four doors, Apollo's unhappy love affairs with Daphne, Hyacinthus, Coronis and Cyparissus. The windows that open out on the back of the house look out upon an exotic ornamental pond fed by a fountain with a charming statue hidden among dwarfed palm trees.

The central hall leads to several other rooms decorated with frescos of grotesques. The two most beautiful are the bedroom furnished with a superb bed from Lucca surmounted by a festooned canopy, decorated with appliqué motifs and sporting bouquets of the same fabric and the small room evoking characters from the Commedia dell' Arte. The owners, having opened the villa to the public, have had to remove most of the furniture because of theft.

The elegant statues placed on the building and scattered throughout the grounds, the graceful ornamental pools and the majestic hall are a clever mixture of 17th-century Mannerist architecture in an 18th-century Classical decor. They reflect the good taste of one of the great families of the region.

The noble alley bordered
by statues celebrating Nature offers
a charming vista.

The entrance hall painted in
trompe-l'œil is highlighted by a
delicately-colored glass chandelier
from Murano.

Grotesques decorate the walls of
the bedroom furnished with a
canopy bed from Lucca.

GARZONI

To the east of Villa Mansi in the small town of Collodi, Villa Garzoni stands at the end of a long line of houses on a wooded hillside. On the right past the San Bartolomeo Church, a road leads through a large portal in the enclosing wall into the legendary gardens. From here, the view of the fabulous composite ensemble, rich in color and shape, is spectacular; it is like looking at a fairy-tale landscape. Originally designed by an skilled amateur architect, Marquis Romano Garzoni, the gardens took almost a century to complete.

In 1328, after the death of Castruccio Castracani, who had ruled over Lucca under the protection of the German emperor, the Garzoni, an old Ghibelline family, were driven out of their city and settled in Collodi on the border between the Luccan and Florentine States. The gardens were begun in 1633 but still did not have a fountain or statue to display at the time of Ferdinand of Austria and Anne de' Medici's visit in 1662; they only reached their final configuration at the end of the century. In 1756, another Romano Garzoni, great-grandson of the first, commissioned the Luccan architect and writer, Ottaviano Diodati, to modify the lower section and to create the hydraulic installations for the fountains.

The bold designers of these grandiose gardens took advantage of the precipitous slope and made creative use of the site to produce a very theatrical effect in the Baroque spirit. A sophisticated succession of terraces linked by a series of monumental staircases stretches up the hillside in symmetrical patterns, on either side of the central axis

The gardens stretch over the slope
on the east side of the house like
an eccentric puzzle; lack of space
prevented them from being laid
out directly below.

The extravagant parterres of the first section assemble
all the elements of a Tuscan garden, evergreen animals,
spiraled bushes and battlemented walls of box hedges,
hollowed out to house statues; a triumph of the topiary art
of the 17th century.

commanding the whole composition. The foreground with its gravel-covered esplanade holds two round basins. One is enhanced by water lilies and jets of water, the other offers a pool for graceful white swans. Lovely lacy parterres planted with fuchsia-colored and deep-purple geraniums adorn the ground.

Two remarkable topiary evergreens trimmed into spirals mark the beginning of the central alley which then ascends several steps up a slight rise and abuts the majestic series of symmetrical staircases. Here, both sides of the first flight of stairs are bordered by hedges and potted lemon trees. In the center, two vast parterres abound with a great variety of decorative elements. A mosaic of heather, perennials and pebbles compose—in the finest details—the Garzoni coat of arms. The whole of the first section is enclosed by a high wall of yew hedges pruned into extravagant battlemented shapes and hollowed out at intervals to make room for small benches surrounded by large jars of azaleas or beautiful Baroque statues with mincing attitudes.

Elegant brick-colored balustrades confine the stairs, and a patterned mosaic decorates the sustaining walls. The two lower landings lengthen into parallel walks invisible from below. The first walk is bordered by palm trees, giving a certain exotic air to the garden. On this first landing, a large rocaille grotto inhabited by a statue of Neptune nestles inside the embankment. The second walk is called the Alley of Pomona. The third level accommodates two gigantic statues of indolent satyrs resting on monumental scrolled consoles at the edge of the woods. Higher up, straight ramps border a cascade where water leaps and bounds over mossy rocks and rough stones and runs down the slope past two enormous stone allegories personifying Florence and Lucca. These rival cities face each other, their hands holding cornucopias out of which water flows; the emblematic animals of both cities lie at their feet. At the culminating point of the prospect, an allegory of Fame blowing into a seashell reigns over a lily-filled basin; the statue's stone wings and drapery flutter against a background of greenery. From this spot looking down over the cascade, a stunning vista framed by trees reveals the parterres of the lower garden and extends towards the outline of the near-by hills.

Past a statue of a wild boar, the Pomona walk leads to a marvelous green theater hidden behind by high hedges pruned into pawn-like shapes. The theater lies under the protection of two stone figures representing Comedy and Tragedy (Thalia and Melopomene), each brandishing emblematic artifacts—the mask and the crown. Beyond the theater, a romantic suspended bridge crosses over a bubbling stream into a strange bamboo forest. A path follows leading into an intricate maze designed to detain lovers within its hedges for just the right amount of time. All these mischievous contrivances bring to mind visions of a life devoid of hardship, filled with elegance and beauty, of merry picnics, of musical entertainment where all ladies

Following page left:
The Basin of Fame marks out the summit of the garden.

Following page right:
Plan of the Garzoni garden in the 17th century after J.C. Shepherd and G.A. Jellicoe, Italian Gardens of the Renaissance, London 1986:
1) entrance, 2) parterre, 3) basin, 4) palm tree walk, 5) monumental stairs 6) Pomona walk, 7) green theater, 8) woods, 9) cascade, 10) Fame Basin, 11) ramps leading to the house.

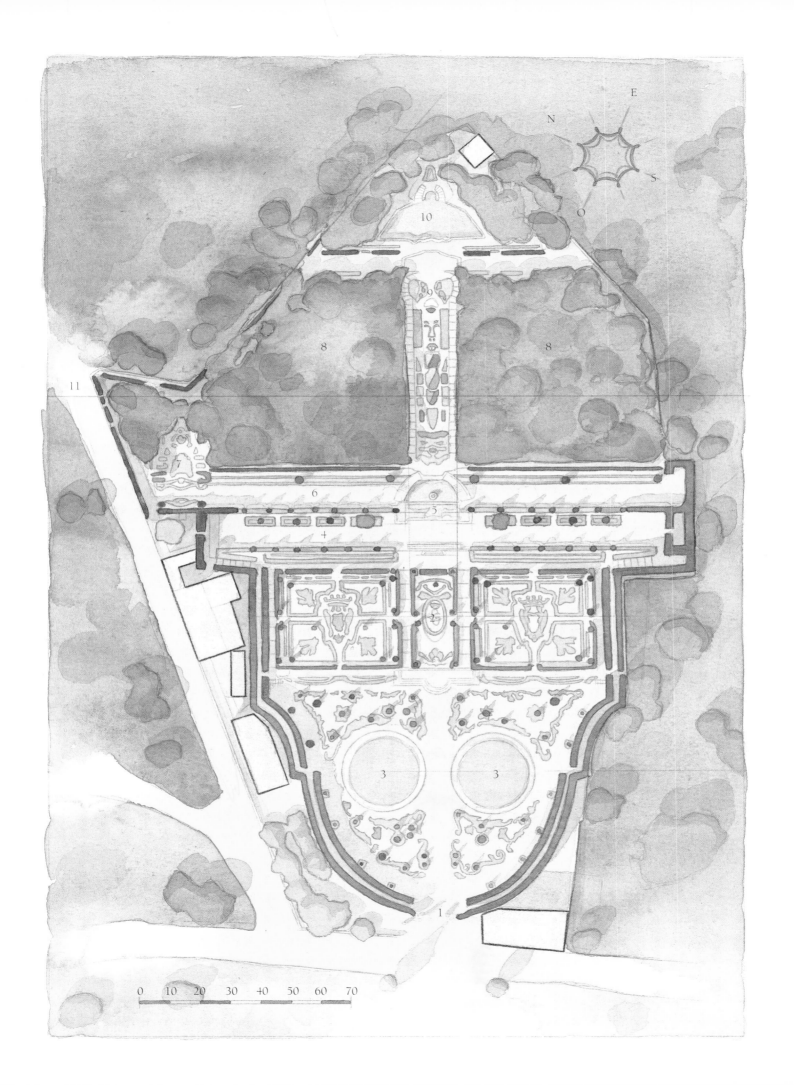

The first-floor gallery covered
by a barrel vault is still paved with
traditional varnished red bricks
from Impruneta.

are bewitching and all gentlemen charming, a society clothed in
precious silks without looking ostentatious, where laughter spills from
every corner.

Beyond the maze, a covered bridge precedes an alley opening
onto a paved esplanade in front of the house. From this magnificent
viewpoint, unfold the garden, the town of Collodi with the massive
San Bartolomeo Church in the foreground and, in the distance, the hills
dotted with olive groves of the Val di Nievole. A wide ramp that used to
accommodate horses and carriages runs down from the courtyard to
the town. The villa was built at the same time as the gardens on the site
of an ancient fortified castle. The majestic building's long façade is articulated by many simply-framed windows and by horizontal, projecting
string courses that underline the separation of each of the four stories.
The slightly higher central block is surmounted by an small elegant
aedicule topped itself by a bell and dispensing an upright thrust to
this long expanse. White fabric blinds protecting the windows from
the midday sun wave in the breeze, giving the façade a theatrical
appearance.

The music and ballroom bear
witness to Marquis Garzoni's
glorious epoch.

The Luccan Baroque style juxtaposed real sculpture and trompe-l'œil: a marble cherub on the banister faces a painted putto in the architectural decor.

Right:
The play of concave and convex volumes of the rococo pavilion enhanced with a mosaic of pebbles.

The portal over which the Garzoni coat of arms is affixed, leads into a vaulted hall opening up on an inner courtyard. At the far end, a terraced wall housing sunken rocaille niches with fountains closes off the area. Above the embankment sits a curious rococo summer pavilion with an intricate curved shape providing a protective screen between the villa and the overhanging houses of the town. This folly, born from Diodati's ingenuity at the end of the 18th century, displays a decaying bright-red façade that has been patinated by the passage of time.

To the left, under the house's portico, lies a straight staircase providing access to the first floor. The walls of the hallway are covered with a complex architectural decor in trompe l'œil which creates an irresistible illusion of unending space by the repetition of mock vaults and the expert handling of perspective.

On the next level, there is a lovely gallery entirely painted with pale-yellow frescos representing antique ruins, still lifes and country landscapes. Parallel to this sunny gallery runs a series of linked rooms. One of the most remarkable of these is the Venetian-style green room furnished with a lovely Luccan canopy bed and doors covered with panels of hand-embroidered silk. The sumptuous music and ballroom is surmounted by an other illusionist trompe-l'œil painting with elaborate perspectives, devised by Angelo Michele Colonna. The vast kitchen is reminiscent of the time when a certain young man, who happened to be the grandson of the villa's cook, told stories about Pinocchio to flabbergasted kitchen boys. The story teller, Carlo Lorenzini, became the town's most famous native son and has been known since then by the name of Collodi.

So widespread was the reputation of the gardens and so great the care bestowed upon them by the Garzoni up to the beginning of this century that they never lost their splendor. Never perhaps have the drawbacks of a natural site been used to such advantage. Romano Garzoni's bold layout of imaginative motifs and his clever handling of scenic inventions allow the formal gardens to gradually merge into the sylvan surroundings. Villa Garzoni is one of the most spectacular Baroque settings of 17th-century Italy.

The front façade of Villa Cetinale.

In the 14th century the Republic of Siena covered a vast territory that stretched to the south of the city past Grosseto and to the east to Chiusi. The city, a Ghibelline (imperial) stronghold, had been under the political and military domination of Florence since the end of the 13th century when the Guelf (papal) forces finally triumphed. While the Sienese bankers and merchants were trying to establish their social and economical influence, the land owners prospered from the resources of the vineyards and the olive groves of the well-known Chianti region. As early as the 11th century, monks like the Vallombrosian Benedictines from Badia a Coltibuono and gentleman farmers like the Ricasoli from Brolio cultivated their land to make a living. But the city of Siena fell victim to fratricidal struggles between the rival Monti families or clans. The internal and external political crisis involving the domination of the Florentine armies over the cities on the border between the two States brought about a decline in commerce and trade starting in the 14th century. The agricultural estates, however, were able to multiply in a countryside that asserted its economical weight over the city. The simple *casa colonica* (farm house) largely fulfilled the owner's needs, except in times of strife, when it was safer to be barricaded behind the walls of a fortified castle.

At the end of the 15th century, Pandolfo Petrucci supported by the Aragonese took advantage of the Medici exile and took power in Siena. This period of relative calm was followed by the Imperial protectorate of the city after Charles V's arrival in Italy in 1530, and Sienese independence came to an end in 1557. When Siena was annexed to the Grand Duchy of Tuscany, the reassured villa owners began to consider refurbishing their country estates and had the old fortified buildings or *case coloniche* reconstructed or torn down. The great Sienese architect of the period was Baldassare Peruzzi who, after having designed the palace of Massimo alle Colonne and the Villa Farnesina in Rome, returned to his birthplace in 1527. He designed several country houses including Belcaro, Celsa, Santa Colomba, Anqua, L'Apparita, Vicobelle and Le Volte Alte; the last two were built for the Chigi, a rich merchant banking family. Peruzzi's constructions, characterized by a purity of proportion, the use of the regional brick, and a taste for perspective and scenographic games exercised a strong influence on other Sienese architects. Even the Baroque Roman architect, Carlo Fontana copied Peruzzi's model for Villa Centinale in the 17th century.

Most of the Sienese villas follow the principles laid down by Peruzzi. They can be distinguished from other Tuscan villas by their extreme simplicity, their lack of ornamentation, their use of ancient materials, like uncut stone or brick, and by their association with medieval architecture.

Badia a Coltibuono an ancient abbey transformed into
a secluded villa in the 19th century; the chapel and the bell
tower are the oldest remaining elements.

Opposite:
Badia a Coltibuono is surrounded by a forest of fir, oak,
and chestnut trees kept up in the 11th century by Benedictine
monks of the Vallombrosian order who also planted the vines
and olive groves.

BADIA A COLTIBUONO

Northeast of Siena, not far from Gaiole in the Chianti region, Badia a Coltibuono rises solemnly against the foothills of the Chianti mountains.

The former abbey, lost in a dense forest of fir trees, exudes an monastic austerity which is heightened by the pervasive stillness and the timeless silence of the surrounding countryside. Seen from afar, the bare walls of rough white stone barely interrupted by windows are dominated by a crenellated campanile. The walk up the winding path deepens the strange impression of having reached the end of the world.

Past the outbuildings, the church appears in back of an airy porch supported by large pillars and with projecting eaves from a sloping tile roof. In this old sanctuary, the priest still celebrates masses and marriages. The church and the adjoining oratory were built in 770 under the auspices of Geremia dei Firidolfi, a Florentine nobleman who found the site ideal for prayer. Monks began to settle there, but the church was soon destroyed by a fire. Rebuilt in 1058 on a Romanesque plan, it was consecrated by Pope Nicholas II.

The abbey was subsequently occupied by Benedictines from Vallombrosa, near Florence. The monks, faithful to their founder's doctrine, San Giovanni Gualberto, began to cultivate the adjoining fields and tend the surrounding forest of fir, oak, and chestnut trees.

In 1427, Abbot Paolo da Montemignaio began constructing a cloister with an upper gallery which led to the small cells of the monks. The cloister, accessible only from inside the church, was restored in the 18th century, and only a few engaged columns from the original building still remain.

The simple stone façade of the monastery was built of rubble masonry. The architectural details, such as the rusticated doorway, the central balcony supported by solid brackets, the ground-floor windows with iron lattice-work and with architraves and sills resting on sturdy consoles, are in keeping with the ascetic character of the place. In 1710, two wings were added, as well as another set of walls, thus forming a sloping paved courtyard closed off by farm buildings at the far end.

In 1810, the peaceful life of the abbey was interrupted after seven centuries by Napoleon I who, by a peremptory edict, ordered the eviction of the monks. Badia a Coltibuono, however, was lucky not to have been destroyed after its closing. It was preserved by the various later owners who were respectful of its religious origin; in particular, the Poniatowski and the Giuntini families, which transformed it into a place of residence.

The interior of the former abbey has nothing in common with the lifestyle of a monastic order and is comfortably appointed as a private house. The refectory was transformed into a living room, furnished with simple wooden chairs and tables, discreet lamps, overstuffed chairs covered in an off-white fabric. The sedate decor harmonizes perfectly with the groin-vaulted ceiling resting on corbels bearing the Giuntini coat of arms and the cycle of dark-toned frescos on the walls, executed by the Mannerist painter Bernardino Poccetti. The medallions bear Latin inscriptions and depict the twelve abbots who ruled the monastery. Other frescoes narrate episodes from the life of Saint Lawrence, the patron saint of Coltibuono. During the summer season, the current owners organize classical music concerts for their friends and neighbors.

The monks' cells on the ground floor have been turned into guest bedrooms. They open out onto a wood-beamed corridor paved in red tile with a herringbone motif. This passageway, decorated with a few painting, displays an important fresco influenced by the Flemish school representing the Crucifixion with the Virgin, Mary Magdalene, Saints Lawrence and Giovanni Gualberto, attributed to the 16th-century master Francesco D'Ubertino, known as Il Bacchiacca.

The white kitchen, with its lovely beamed ceiling is equipped with a marble-covered wooden counter and displays of hanging copper pots. The owner, an excellent cook, gives lessons in Tuscan gastronomy using local products, since farming lives on at Badia. Wine, oil and *grappa*, an eau-de-vie made from grapes, are still produced according to ancestral methods handed down by the 11th-century monks.

Behind the abbey two paved terraces on different levels overlook the garden that descends towards the outside walls. The lower one is decorated with a rustic stonework fountain with a large basin. On the side of the garden bordered by ivy-covered farmhouses, a magnificent magnolia tree provides shade for the wooden benches set under its branches. Farther away, separated by a low wall, beds of box-hedge topiary trimmed into cones and other geometric shapes share the company of lovely ivory-colored Banks roses around a small square basin with a stone rim. In the background lavender bushes and fruit trees blossom in the orchard. This garden is protected by high walls

The rough stone façade of the monastery with its rusticated entrance; its austere appearance has endured since the 15th century in spite of a few architectural additions.

Pergolas laden with vines divide
the garden creating many small
cloistered areas reminiscent of
monastic cells.

built during the Renaissance. The pergolas, perfectly designed for private conversation, offer a retreat from prying eyes. In the distance, the deep forest of fir trees provides a suitable backdrop for contemplation.

Badia a Coltibuono is an rare example of an old abbey transformed into a villa in the 19th century. The cloister-like atmosphere and a respect for tradition has been maintained making a soothing and restful dwelling.

An ideal spot for meditation, the garden
with its rhythmical patterns of green and
white blends in perfectly with the
vineyards, olive groves and forest in the
distance.

Through the ages, the mighty villa-fortress of Brolio resisted repeated assaults by Sienese and Imperial armies. Today it watches over the Ricasoli family's wine-making enterprise, which produces of the savory Chianti Classico.

Right:
View from the road of the fortress with its Neo-Gothic, brick-clad palazzo restored in the 19th century, contrasting with the gray stone of the ramparts raised by Giuliano da Sangallo during the Renaissance.

BROLIO

A little to the south of Badia a Coltibuono and to the northeast of Siena, the fantastic indomitable Castello di Brolio looms over the plain. It is perched on a small hill among gray-green vineyards and olive groves dominating the yellow fields and the dark-green forests of pine and fir in the heart of the Chianti Classico wine region. In 1847, Baron Bettino Ricasoli created the renowned Gallo Nero label. The world famous wine is produced on the 62 acres of flourishing vineyards around the castle, which is still owned by the same family.

The fortress, bristling with watchtowers and bartizans barely visible through the surrounding foliage, has belonged to the Ricasoli family since the 11th century. The history of the castle is a very bloody one indeed. Built around 1000 A.D., it was an outpost of the Florentines and therefore subjected to many attacks by Sienese troops. In 1432, Antonio Petrucci, the great Sienese strategist, successfully breached the walls of the stronghold. Only a few years later, however, the Florentines won it back again. In 1452, Ferdinand I, Duke of Calabria, son of the King of Naples, conducted an assault on the castle with his Aragonese troops, but to no avail. It was not until 1478 that the fortress again changed hands. The Sienese took their revenge on the castle that had defied them for so long by completely destroying it. In 1484, the Ricasoli family, who had never abandoned their property, built it back up during the period of peace established by Lorenzo de' Medici. They entrusted the reconstruction of the bulwarks, as we see

Above the ramparts, a vast
esplanade with a winter garden
forms a terrace in front of the
castle.

them today, to Giuliano da Sangallo, who had already engineered the fortifications at Sarzana. The walls reinforced at the corners by bastions are approximately 50 ft. high and surround the building for a total perimeter of about 1500 ft. In 1529, Spanish soldiers from the Imperial army launched a successful attack on the castle but were chased away, in turn, the next year when the Medici returned to power. It then remained in Florentine hands.

A rocky path winding through a dank forest of cypresses and running along the high curtain walls provides access to the rear of the castle. The gloomy atmosphere of the trail is not very reassuring and when the visitor finally reaches the gate he almost expects the sound of the bell to bring out a grisly, hunch-backed servant from another age. Beyond the gate, a broad and winding ramp that was hammered smooth by horses' hooves and carriage wheels leads up to the castle itself. Bettino Ricasoli, the "iron baron" who succeeded Cavour at the head of the government and contributed to the unification of Italy, hired the architect Pietro Marchetti to reface the main block of the building with a covering of deep red bricks in the Neo-Gothic style, imitating the old Sienese buildings. This surface treatment does not shock, however, and blends stylistically with the other older edifices of the complex.

The family chapel to the left, laid out in a simple rectangular plan with walls of bare stone, dates back to 1348. The interior is decorated with fresco medallions of saints. The chancel is adorned with mosaics and the ribbed ceiling with ornamental motifs. A back door in the chancel leads to a paved courtyard above which looms the medieval stone keep pierced with loopholes and protected from assailants by merlons and crenels. This is where the Ricasoli family took refuge when their enemies broke through the first ramparts around the castle.

Along an esplanade decorated with geometric plantations, the attractive Neo-Gothic section of the castle with its huge central block and smaller lateral wings features a delicate overhanging turret. A succession of mullioned lancet windows and two small balconies supported by finely sculpted corbels enliven the façade. The crenellations that crown the building duplicate those of the keep. All of these details give the ensemble a refined and graceful aspect that contrasts with the more massive style of the older buildings. The architect accomplished his Neo-Gothic scheme to perfection, yet without detracting from the character of the medieval fortress, and created a strong theatrical effect. Although very different in atmosphere, it is reminiscent of Louis II of Bavaria's fantastic Neuschwanstein Castle.

From the esplanade running along the façade of the central section of the castle there is a grand view of the Chianti hills glowing in the distance. It is surprising to discover beneath Sangallo's solid curtain walls an extraordinary formal Italian garden with potted plants and boxwood bordering smooth lawns laid out in geometrical patterns. The precise design and the lush green color of this composition stand out against the gray walls and the gray-green olive groves. Past several flower beds bordering a stone winter garden with arched-windows, the esplanade ends at an old ivy-covered turret, a look-out post on which the guards made their rounds.

The interior of the house has been restored in the same taste as the exterior. The rooms are decorated with frescos depicting scenes from the Middle Ages against a gold background. The coffered ceilings are painted with geometric motifs. Huge stone fireplaces, embroidered wallcoverings, coats of arms, standards and armor complete the setting. The furniture matches the decor. The large wooden chests and tables and the high-backed leather-covered chairs are reminiscent of medieval times, yet several rooms, like the small red *salotto* and the green room, retain the austere 15th-century Tuscan style.

Splendid formal Italian-style gardens, a comfortable and remodelled 19th-century residence within fortified walls combined with a working winery make Castello di Brolio one of the most original of the Sienese estates. It can be considered a true villa in all senses of the word, and a sign on the ramparts says as much.

Central motif of the formal garden.

Above:
On the left the family chapel and on the right the keep, both from the original 14th-century fortress.

Opposite:
In the 19th century, a striking formal Italian garden replaced the moats; olive groves and vineyards cover the Chianti hills in the distance.

Villa Anqua has preserved an agricultural setting, remaining faithful to the principles developed by L. B. Alberti on how harmony should reign between architecture and nature.

Right:
The cypress-bordered road and the umbrella pines leading to the esplanade in front of the villa.

ANQUA

Villa Anqua is situated in a small town bearing the same name to the southwest of Siena between Castelnuovo and Radicondoli at the edge of the Sienese province. The estate can be seen from afar perched on a little hill in the middle of an agricultural complex surrounded by fields with grazing horses and farm land.

Past several outbuildings along a cypress-bordered road, a tiny brick-colored church rests on a sleepy esplanade under the shade of umbrella pines. It supports a pointed roof and is pierced by an œil-de-bœuf above the entranceway, surmounted by a 17th-century Latin cross over a Baroque open pediment. To the right, several roughly-carved steps mount a paved alley with a central run-off gutter for rain water and lead to a low crenellated wall crowned by slender merlons supporting stone balls. From this spot, the garden is visible through the embrasures.

The esplanade is flanked by an outbuilding bearing the coat of arms of the Pannochieschi d'Elci: two eagles, back to back, crowned with the Maltese Cross and a plumed helm. The old Sienese family, whose palace proudly sits on the Piazza del Campo in Siena, has always owned Villa Anqua. This structure, made of variegated rough stones, is lengthen by a wall and pierced with a rusticated arch, also surmounted by brick merlons crowned with balls. A fine wrought-iron gate opens into a lovely enclosed courtyard decorated with a herringbone-pattern brick pavement and marked by lines of white

The depiction of the properties acquired by the Pannochieschi d'Elci is reminiscent of the panoramas of the Medici villas painted by Giusto Utens.

Above:
The simple Pannochieschi d'Elci chapel underlined by several rows of white stone.

Opposite:
View of the enclosed garden and the rolling fields beyond at the end of the paved alley skirting the chapel.

stone. Here, a lovely highly-stylized Renaissance well embellishes the setting, its wrought-iron railing pounded into intricate scrolls and fleur-de-lys. On the right, stands the elegant residence built in the 16th century by Baldassare Peruzzi. The beautifully-proportioned façade entirely covered with a small regular brick facing, worthy of a Sienese palace, seems somewhat out of place in the middle of such a rustic setting. A few architectural elements were added in the 17th century such as the architraves of the simple, white stone trabeated windows marked with the family's coat of arms, the string courses that underline the separation between the stories, the rusticated door frame and the large escutcheon of the Pannochieschi d'Elci. These pure lines make a harmonious ensemble echoed by the equally lovely proportions of the granary on the other side of the courtyard. This older edifice built of a variety of stones is adorned with square windows and an identical doorway.

Inside, the rather solemn house has preserved the beautiful frescos on the barrel and groin-vaulted ceiling of the first floor. These display picturesque scenes of mock pergolas and mascarons. The painted lunettes on one of the vaults present an inventory of the numerous possessions of the family (the fortified castle of Perolla, Montemassi, Tirli and Elci) as if to reaffirm the political power of the Pannochieschi d'Elci. On the ground floor, the kitchen exhibits copper pots and iron pans in good repair from an earlier period and has a beautiful beamed ceiling dressed with a colorful variety of grotesque motifs.

Across from the entrance through another crenellated wall lies the junction of the garden's two vine-covered pergolas; one of them resting on brick pillars, the other on simple wooden beams. The two alleys, set at right angles and bound by a trellis of climbing roses and several boxwood hedges trimmed into bench-like shapes, produce an impressive effect of perspective with all their converging lines.

Anqua, in spite of its veritable city-type architecture, has kept the rustic appearance of a large farm surrounded by outbuildings and other dwellings and remains almost unchanged since the 16th century.

The façade of the granary
mirroring the house.

Above left:
Entrance to the villa;
the juxtaposition of the rough
stone surface of the outbuilding
with the regular brick façade of the
16th-century house creates
a harmonious and peaceful
ensemble.

The simple enclosed garden
resembles those preferred by the
Tuscan Humanists.

Above right:
The white stone window and door
frames highlight the warm brick
color of this lovely façade.

Opposite:
The owners have chosen an
unsophisticated and cozy setting
for their small salon.

The admirable rosy façade of the house and the boxwood
parterre decorated by large voluptuous statues displaying
cornucopias. To the right in the background, the silhouette of
the pigeon loft among the olive trees.

Right:
The villa hidden among the houses of Cetinale.

CETINALE

Villa Cetinale is hidden among houses in a town bearing the same name on a hillside to the west of Siena near Sovicille. Behind a wrought-iron gate lies a little garden facing an elegant beautifully-proportioned façade.

The house was constructed in 1680 by the great Baroque architect Carlo Fontana for Cardinal Flavio Chigi, nephew of Pope Alexander VII. This family of rich Sienese bankers established their influence over Rome in the 15th century in the service of the pope. The Chigi family multiplied their estates and commissioned the greatest artists to work for them in Rome (Palazzo Chigi by Giacomo della Porta and Maderna, Villa Farnesina by Baldassare Peruzzi and Raphael, Bernini's Piazza S. Pietro) and in the neighborhood of Siena (Villa Le Volte Alte and Villa Vicobello by Peruzzi). In 1691, Cardinal Chigi entertained Cosimo III at Cetinale with all the honors due to a Grand Duke.

Fontana elaborated on Peruzzi's U-shaped plan—a cube with two wings projecting from the principal façade—for Le Volte Alte (1492) as well as the even more refined La Farnesina (1505). A plan using the ground floor for utilitarian purposes while placing the reception rooms above-stairs is a typical Roman architectural device not found in most Tuscan villas which open onto the gardens level. As in all of Peruzzi's designs, the ground-floor arches form a portico whereas those on the next level are blind and only frame the windows. Fontana adopted this same disposition for the first and second stories of the

Potted plants and ivy on the façade
enliven the building. To the north,
the long cypress walk leading
to the hermitage.

Below:
Detail of the boxwood parterre in
front of the green house.

central block. The ensemble is surmounted by an attic with small windows just beneath the roof. He added decorative elements that give the façade a more Baroque appearance: the delicate brick frames of the windows and arches borne on pillars, the majestic coats of arms above the second story and the string-course between the different levels. These architectural motifs and the contrasting play between the cream color of the smooth rendering, the rosy-brick frames and the light gray of the corner stones give the building a feeling of gentleness and serenity.

The central alley leads through a parterre of strangely-shaped boxwood trimmed into conic and cubic shapes, enhanced by lemon trees in terra cotta urns. Low ivy-clad green houses form a backdrop for statues. Directly to the right of the villa, two rows of box bushes lead to a little chapel built on a simple plan, whose entrance door is surmounted by a segmental pediment and crowned by a large triangular gable. Its pure lines are underlined by the same rosy brick as the façade of the main house.

Potted trees and beds of flowers are the only reminders of the 17th-century parterre in front of the rear façade. A monumental staircase of definite Baroque style with a double flight of steps provides access to a mezzanine before reaching the first floor. Details like the balustrade, the œils-de-bœuf pierced through both flanks of the stairs, the two arches that repeat the alignment of the south façade

The rear façade is dominated by a monumental staircase crowned by rusticated pilasters, Alexander VII's papal coat of arms and the triangular pediment. On the left the small brick-covered chapel.

and the majestic frame of the central door greatly enhance the building.

To the east of the house, behind the supporting wall surmounted by antique busts, an olive orchard spreads out in a succession of terraces dominated by the elegant silhouette of a pigeon loft. Delicately covered with a brick facing and adorned with a clock, this structure opens onto an arcade where cooing doves come to roost.

A long, straight grassy walk between a row of high cypress trees leads to a fabulous gateway flanked by two extravagant brick piers crowned by stone busts and pyramidal finials. The piers have been hollowed out with niches to house strange figures wearing phrygian bonnets, their arms crossed over their breasts. These are the silent guardians announcing the entrance to another world. From this spot, an unforgettable prospect spreads forth cutting through the olive groves and the wild romantic woods beyond, where a steep irregular flight of stone steps—the Scala Santa—ascends the slope to a hermitage on the crest of the hill. The building, with a Lorraine cross embedded in the façade, is adorned with square niches, each containing the bust of a saint. The vast ilex forest is scattered with Baroque statues by Bartolomeo Mazzuoli and several small chapels. Cardinal Chigi named these woods *The Thebaid* in reference to the Egyptian deserts in which, in the 3rd century A. D., many Christians took refuge from persecutions and led lives of seclusion. The cardinal, seeking a retreat where he could repent for murdering a rival in a fit of jealousy, used to make a daily pilgrimage up the hill to unburden his soul, in hopes of earning his way to paradise.

Villa Cetinale is highlighted by an extraordinary *mise en scène* around an axis that begins to the south of the entrance of the villa, crosses the property and continues on through orchards and woods to the hermitage, producing a startling visual effect of distance and grandeur. The layout is a simple but admirable, taking advantage of a natural site to complete the perspective.

The brick piers, the strict alignment of cypress trees and the
arches of the façade produce a startling perspective.

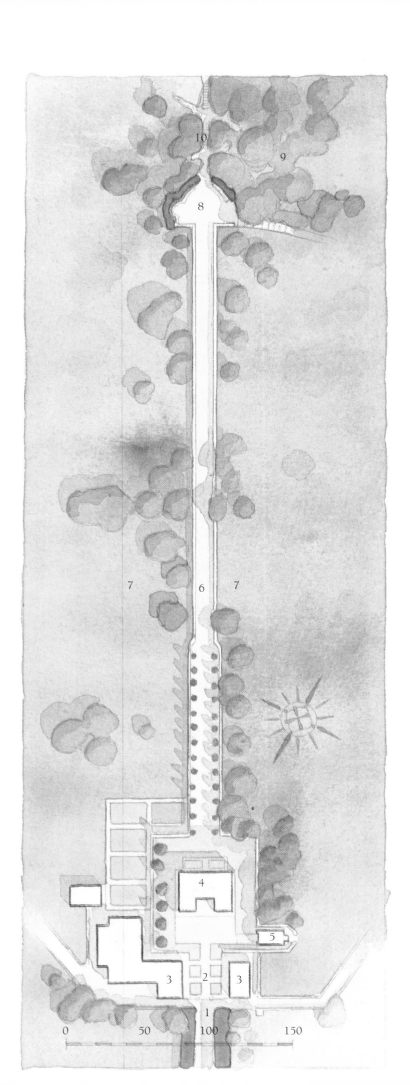

Left:
The plan of Villa Cetinale in the 17th century after J. C. Shepherd and G. A. Jellicoe, Italian Gardens of the Renaissance. London: 1986.

1) entrance, 2) parterre, 3) greenhouses, 4) house, 5) chapel, 6) cypress walk, 7) olive groves, 8) clearing, 9) woods, 10) stairs.

Above and right:
Cardinal Flavio Chigi's "Way of the Cross" through the forest of the Thebaid, a spectacular scenic prospect linking the house to the hermitage.

The architecture of L'Apparita belongs to the traditional style
of Siena, but appears both modern and sparing.

L'APPARITA

Villa L'Apparita is situated near the town of Santa Maria, in the midst of rolling hills dotted with flocks of grazing sheep. Set in the middle of an open field, the unadorned edifice is built of very fine-gauge brick. The villa has served both as farmhouse and residence but its most interesting feature is its distinctive two-tiered portico, constructed as free-standing loggias by Baldassare Peruzzi in the 16th century, probably for visual pleaure alone. This extravagance also applied to the lavish entertainment so much in vogue at the time. The upper loggia, which is suggestive of a theater stage and seems to exist merely for its aesthetic value, offers sweeping vistas of the lush landscape. Only the pilasters projecting slightly from the facade of the upper level enliven the pure lines of the structure, giving it a scenographic quality. The rear portion of the building with its small windows was added later and constructed in the same brickwork. The straight staircase, instead of taking an axial position in the middle of a façade, rises on one side of the villa, without disturbing the rhythm of the arcades.

On the other side, an ivy-framed entrance opens onto a main hall. The interior space of this composite room unfolds beneath four arches spreading out from a single pillar. Architectural elements tend to take precedence over the discreet furnishings that have been chosen in perfect harmony with the stark character of the ensemble. On the first floor, a long hall bordered by six wooden columns with Corinthian capitals lends an almost monastic atmosphere to the interior.

Above:
Peruzzi's distinctive façade changes color throughout the day, from a rose beige to an intense red in the evening, like a theater changing its scenery.

The vast empty field in front of the villa emphasizes its brooding austerity.

Here, the Sienese lawyer and present owner of L'Apparita, Giovanni Guiso, has assembled a precious collection of miniature theaters from all over the world, complete with tiny puppets in front of hand-painted and meticulously detailed sets. On special occasions, he delights his friends with performances of lyric operas, such as *Manon, Il Trovatore, Madame Butterfly* and *The Magic Flute*....

The estate seems entirely devoted to the stage, for Don Guiso has set up an open-air theater facing the beautiful Chianti hills in a vast field dotted with cypress and pomegranate trees and broom, blackberry, lavender bushes, all around the villa. A semi-circle of brown wooden benches faces the green stage. The entrance is marked by two delicately-carved terra cotta vases with handles in the form of swan's necks and mounted on pedestals decorated with grotesques. More vases outline the stage which is bounded by a circle of stones embedded in the lawn. A hedge of bushes serves as natural back-drop for this small amphitheater. The intense raw sienna color of the vases contrasts with the lush green of the lawn and echoes the red brick of the villa. Here, in the summer, Don Guiso holds poetry readings and music performances. In 1960, this highly stylized yet simple space was planned by Pietro Porcinai, the same landscape architect who designed the gardens of Gamberaia and Il Roseto. He succeeded in exploiting the novelty of Peruzzi's original construction and integrating it into a theatrical complex.

Affixed to a low brick wall in the garden of the villa is an inscribed quotation from *L'Aminta* by Torquato Tasso that truly describes Don Guiso's philosophy: "All time not spent in loving is lost." The owner has succeeded in giving us a taste of paradise. This villa is a delight to the spirit, in the manner of the Renaissance imagined by the Humanists.

A harmony and purity of line enfold the villa in an atmosphere of serenity and poetry. It is a quiet world given over to the worship of beauty and the arts. L'Apparita as a whole bears little of the traditional features of a Tuscan villa and for this reason is an exception that deserves particular attention.

Preceding left and opposite:
The green stage looking out at the Chianti hills. Porcinai has successfully created a spectacular space by juxtaposing elements of the greatest simplicity.

PRACTICAL INFORMATION

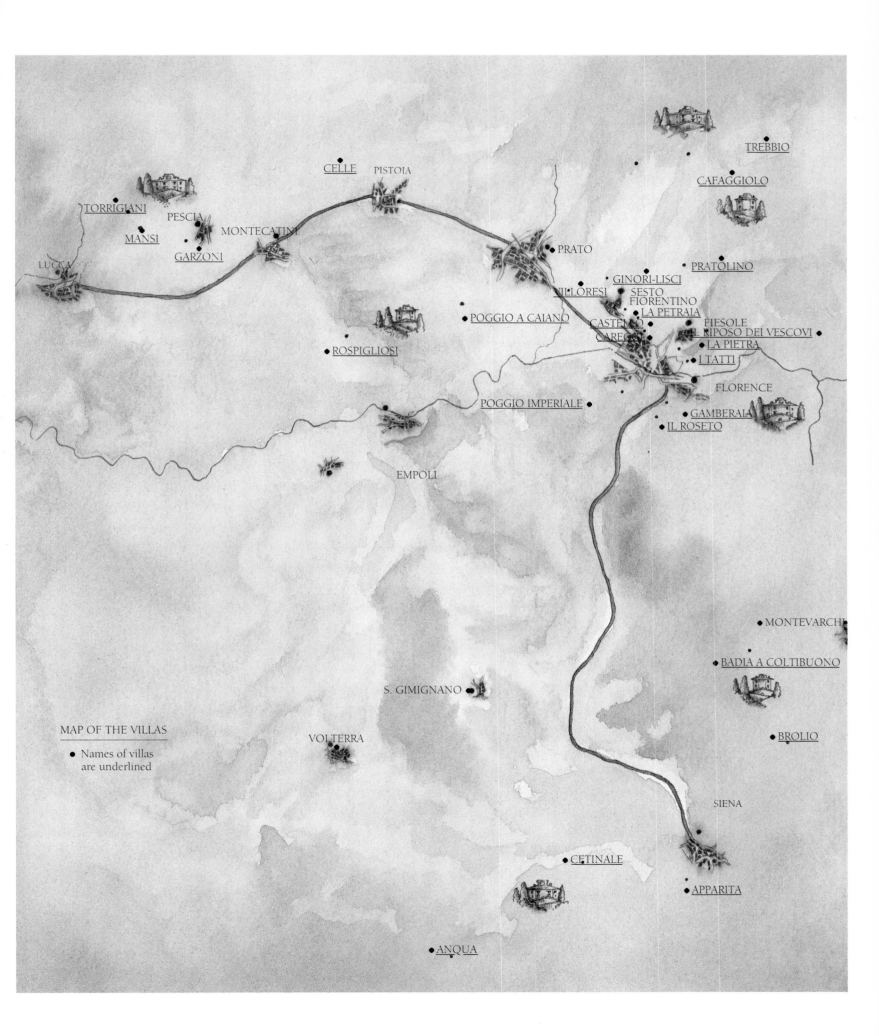

TREBBIO

CELLE PISTOIA

CAFAGGIOLO

TORRIGIANI

PESCIA

MANSI MONTECATINI

PRATOLINO

GARZONI

GINORI-LISCI

LUCCA

VILLORESI SESTO FIORENTINO

PRATO

POGGIO A CAIANO

LA PETRAIA

CASTELLO FIESOLE

CAREGGI IL RIPOSO DEI VESCOVI

ROSPIGLIOSI

LA PIETRA

I TATTI

FLORENCE

POGGIO IMPERIALE

GAMBERAIA

IL ROSETO

EMPOLI

MONTEVARCHI

BADIA A COLTIBUONO

S. GIMIGNANO

MAP OF THE VILLAS

BROLIO

• Names of villas
  are underlined

VOLTERRA

SIENA

CETINALE

APPARITA

ANQUA

INDEX

BIBLIOGRAPHY

1) HISTORICAL OUTLINE

ACTON, Harold. *The Last Medici.* London: Thames and Hudson, 1980 (1st. pub. 1958).

ALBERTI, Leon Battista. *I dieci libri dell'Architecttura.* Milan: 1960 (1st. pub. 1546). Eng. trans. *Ten Books on Architecture.* London: Alec Tiranti, 1965.

BEC, C. *Les Marchands-écrivains, affaires et humanisme à Florence (1375-1434).* Paris: Mouton et Cie, 1967.

BENTMANN, Reinhard and Müller, Michaël. *Die Villa als Herrschaftarchitektur.* Frankfurt am Main: Suhrkamp, 1970.

BOCCACCIO, Giovanni. *Decameron,* tr. by G. H. McWilliam. New York: Penguin, 1972.

BORTOLOTTI, L. *Siena.* Rome: Laterza, 1983.

CARUNCHIO, T. *Origine della villa rinascimentale.* Rome: Bulzoni, 1974.

CHASTEL, André. *Art et humanisme à Florence au temps de Laurent le Magnifique.* Paris: PUF, 1982.

COLONNA, Francesco. *Hypnerotomachia Poliphili.* Venice: Aldo Manucio, 1499. *The Strife of Love in a Dreame,* reprint Delmar, NY: Schol Facsimiles, 1973.

D'ADDARIO, A. *La formazione dello stato moderno in Toscana da Cosimo il Vecchio a Cosimo I de' Medici.* Lecce: Adriatica, 1976.

DIAZ, F. "Il granducato di Toscana. I Medici," in *Storia d'Italia,* vol. XIII, t. I. Turin: U.T.E.T. 1976.

FALCONE, Giuseppe. *La nuova vaga e dilettevole villa.* Brescia: Buozola, 1559.

FARA, A. *Buontalenti, achitettura e teatro.* Florence: La Nuova Italia, 1979.

GALLO, Agostino. *Le Vinti Giornate dell'agricoltura et de'piaceri della villa.* Venice: G. Percaccino, 1569.

HEYDENREICH, L. H. "La villa: genesi e sviluppi fino al Palladio," in *Bollettino C. I. S. A. Andrea Palladio,* XI, 1969.

INGHIRAMI, F. *Storia della Toscana.* 17 vols. Fiesole: Poligrafia fiesolana, 1841-1843.

MARCHINI, G. *Giuliano da Sangallo.* Florence: Sansoni, 1942.

MORISANI, O. *Michelozzo achitetto.* Turin: G. Einaudi, 1951.

PATZAK, B. *Palast und Villa in Toscana.* Leipzig: Klinkhardt und Biermann, 1908-1913.

PERRENS, F. T. *Histoire de Florence depuis la domination des Mèdicis jusqu'à la chute de la République (1434 - 1531).* 3 Vols. Paris: Quantin, 1888-1890.

PLINY THE YOUNGER. *Letters.* 2 vols. Loeb Classics. Cambridge: Havard University Press.

RENOUARD, Y. *Les hommes d'affaires italiens du Moyen Age.* Paris: Armand Colin, 1968.

ROSS, J. *Lives of the Early Medici as Told in Their Correspondance.* Boston: 1911.

SCHIAPPARELLI, A. *La casa fiorentina e i suoi arredi nei secoli XIV e XV.* Florence: 1983.

SPINI, G., ed. *Architecttura e politica da Cosimo I a Ferdinado.* Florence: Olschki, 1976.

TOMMASI, G. *Sommorio della storia di Lucca.* Lucca: M. Pacini Fazzi, 1969.

YOUNG, G. F. *The Medici.* 2 vols. London: 1909.

2) VILLAS

ACTON, H. *The Villas of Tuscany.* London: Thames and Hudson, 1987 (1st pub. 1973).

AGNELLI, Marella. *Giardini italiani.* Milan: Rizzoli, 1987. *Gardens of the Italians Villas.* tr. from It. New York: Rizzoli Intl. 1987.

ANDREINI GALLI, N. *Ville pistoiesi.* Lucca: Maria Pacini Fazzi, 1989.

ANGUILLESI, G. *Notizie istoriche dei palazzi e ville appartenenti alla I. R. Corona Toscana.* Pisa: N. Capurro, 1815.

BAGATTI-VALSECCHI, P.F. *Ville d'Italia.* Milan: T.C.I., 1974.

BELLI BARSALI, I. *Le ville lucchesi.* Roma: De Luca, 1964.

BORSI, F. and PAMPALONI, G. *Ville e giardini;* Novara: 1984.

CAROCCI, G. *I dintorni di Firenze. Nuova guida-illustrazione storico-artistica.* Florence: Galletti e Cocci, 1906-1907 (1st pub. 1881).

CASTELLUCCI, L. and Scarfiotti, G. L. *Abitare in Toscana: I castelli, le fattorie, le ville, le abbazie.* Milan: Arnoldo Mondadori, 1990.

CLARKE, E. and Bencini, R. *The Gardens of Tuscany.* London: Weidenfeld and Nicholson, 1990.

EBERLEIN, H.D. *Villas of Florence and Tuscany.* Philadelphia: J.B. Lippincott, 1922.

FANFANI, G. *Voci e volti delle ville fiorentine.* Bologna: Forni, 1988 (1st pub. 1939).

LENSI ORLANDI, G. *Le ville di Firenze.* 2 vols. Florence: Vallecchi, 1965 (1st pub. 1954).

MADER, G. and NEUBERT-MADER, L. *Jardins Italiens.* Fribourg: Office du Livre, 1987.

MASSON, Georgina. *Italian Gardens.* London: Thames and Hudson, 1961

MIGNANI, D. *Le ville Medicee di Giusto Utens.* Florence: Arnaud, 1988.

MONTAIGNE, Michel de. *Journal de voyage en Italie par la Suisse et l'Allemagne en 1580 et 1581.* Paris: Gallimard Folio, 1983 (1st pub. 1581). *Travel Journal.* tr. from Fr. by Donald M. Frame. Berkeley: North Point Press, 1983

MORENI, D. *Notizie istoriche dei contorni di Firenze.* 6 vol., Florence: 1791-1795.

REPETTI, E. *Dizionario geografico fisico storico della Toscana contenete la descrizione di tutti i luoghi del Granducato.* 6 vols. Florence: Repetti, 1833-1846.

ROSS, J. *Florentine Villas.* London-New-York: 1911 (1st pub. 1901).

RUGGERI, G. *Piante dei palazzi, ville e giardini del Granducato di Toscana.* Florence: 1742.

SCIOLLA, G. C. "Ville Medicee," in *Le grandi ville italiane,* Novare: Istituto Geografico de Agostini, 1982.

SHEPHERD, J. C. and JELLICOE, G. A. *Italian Gardens of the Renaissance.* London: Academy Ed. 1986 (1st pub. 1925).

TOURING CLUB ITALIANO. *Firenze e dintorni,* Guida d'Italia del Touring Club Italiano. Milan: T. C. I. 1974.

TOURING CLUB ITALIANO. *Toscana,* Guida d'Italia del Touring Club Italiano. Milan: T. C. I. 1974.

VASARI, G. *Le vite de' più eccellenti pittori, scultori et architettori.* Florence: G. C. Sansoni, 1878-1885 (1st. ed. 1550). *Lives of the Most Eminent Painters, Sculptors & Architects.* 10 vols. reprint of 1915. New York: AMS Prints.

VASARI II GIOVANE, G. *La città ideale, piante di chiese (palazzi e ville) di Toscana e d'Italia.* Rome, 1970 (1st pub. 1598).

WARTON, Edith. *Italian Villas and their Gardens.* New York: Da Capo Press, 1976 (1st pub. 1904).

ZANGHERI, L. "Ville della Provincia de Firenze: La città," in *Ville Italiane,* ed. P. F. Bagatti Valsecchi, Vol. Toscana 1. Milan: Rusconi, 1989.

ZOCCHI, G. *Vedute delle ville ed altrio luoghi della Toscana.* Florence: Bouchard, 1744.

Statue representing Apennines
at Villa Castello.